BY
PEGGY SUE HENRY

Beading Patterns and Designs of the Native North American Indian
with Illustrated and Written Instructions

Copyright 1990
Beads to Buckskins Publications
Care of: Jayhawk Rock and Fur Shop

All rights reserved including those to reproduce this book or parts thereof in any form without written permission from publisher.

Contents

Introduction 5
Acknowledgments 7
About the Author 8
Materials Needed 10
Review on Loom Beading 13
Peyote Stitch 28
Squaw Dress Instructions 41
Moccasin Pattern Instructions 45
Brain Tanning Instructions 51
Color Photo Section 57
Cabochon Jewelry Instructions 71
Loom Beading Without a Loom 77
Beaded Fringe 82
Instructions for Beaded Buckles 88
The Brick Stitch 90
The Edge Stitch 94

Introduction

One of the wonderful Aboriginal Arts that exists today is the beadwork of the Native North American Indian.

Beadwork, unlike other textile art, has a greater capacity for enduring the ages. Leather and sinew don't seem to disintegrate as quickly as the cotton or vegetable threads used in garments or the reeds used in baskets.

Glass and stone beads have been excavated that are thousands of years old. Some are still together in the original style of the ornament, which tells me that man has always been a little ostentatious when it comes to adorning his person.

It's human nature to try to make yourself as becoming as possible to other people. Fads and styles of most cultures come and go very quickly, but according to my research of the American Indian, their dress and styles have been traditionally the same for generations. Their garments were made with the idea in mind that they had to last for several seasons. They were designed according to the tribal exception of dress handed down from their ancestors. The style has been proven to withstand the elements and to serve the best purpose and comfort obtainable.

When it came to applying ornament to these garments, is where the individuals styles came in. During times of war, the men would raid other tribes. When they returned home with the ill-fated tribe's treasures, they would divide the booty among the women of their own families. Thus, the interchange of style and competitive adornment begins.

A warrior took great pride in being able to present to his wife and family beads and trinkets to apply to his or their garments. If he had more than one wife, you could tell which one he favored the most by her colorful and sometimes noisy attire she wore to the tribal ceremonies and social get-togethers.

I enjoy being able to recreate something very beautiful that isn't plastic but from an age when man's existence depended on his own personal skills along with those of his tribe. I am of course referring to beadwork and fur and leather garments. I take pleasure in passing on the crafts that have been handed down to me.

Like any other hand or needle work, beading is a matter of practice, so don't be discouraged if your first attempt doesn't look exactly like the one in the picture. It will get better with each project. Beadwork is also great therapy for relaxing and relieving stress, while making something you will enjoy wearing.

I like to think that some of the patterns I do are absolute originals, but each time I think I have created something that nobody else has ever done, I see one similar in a museum or at a pow-wow. Well done beadwork is like a good painting. It is admired and treasured for as long as it lasts.

If you are a beader, I know you are always searching for a new look or pattern. Sometimes this can be achieved simply by changing the color or size of bead or using a crystal for the turn bead on fringe.

In this new series of designs in beadwork I have covered many different styles to satisfy the tastes of the modern beader, while at the same time keeping the traditional patterns active. You will want to acquire all twelve volumes for your collection. Each book in this series is produced with the idea of preserving the old and inspiring new ideas for your own achievement. The color photographs, patterns and directions are presented to generate your own imagination and help develop your talent. I believe you will find the patterns easy to follow.

Beadwork is sweeping the nation in favorable fashion. It is exciting, becoming, and most of all affordable. It offers color and styles for each individual taste. You can be as showy as a diamond or as subtle and elusive as a shaded flower.

Some people look at a nice piece of beadwork and say, "I could never sit still long enough to do that." Well, most usually the person who made the piece did not sit still from the beginning of the project to the end of it either. Like myself, they probably keep a particular project they are working on next to the easy chair or wherever they do spend time sitting and resting during the day or evening. When I take a break and sit down, I pick up my beading and work on it for a few minutes.

If my husband watches T.V. in the evening, I join him and work on my beading. You can get a lot done in an hour each evening.

We travel a lot because of our business, and I do a lot of beading from state to state while my husband drives. The beadwork featured on the front cover of volumes two and three was done while traveling, so I'm not suggesting the impossible. Prove to yourself that you can at least sit still a few minutes at a time over a period of one month to complete one project. You will develop a lot of patience and relieve a great deal of stress. Remember to work under good light. Bad lighting causes mistakes, and too many mistakes discourage you before you have given beading a fair chance. It's also important that you do not start with a pattern so large that it will take forever to finish. Until you have mastered a little coordination of needle and eye, think of small projects, such as earrings or appliques not over three inches in diameter.

Imagine how exciting it would be to have someone ask to pay you a lot of money to make for them a piece of beadwork like the one you created especially for yourself. I am frequently approached when my husband or I wear beadwork.

I encourage you to join me in this craft. You will wonder why you waited to long to give it a try.

Acknowledgments

No. 1 . . . I would like to express my appreciation and thanks to my friends, Frieda Bates, Shalimar Tracey, my sister-in-law, Doris Kennedy, and Jude Biegert, for sharing their beautiful beadwork with us. These ladies have spent a great deal of time on the magnificent show pieces shown in the color section of this book.

No. 2 . . . Photography: Karon McIntyre (API) of Hill City, Ks., and Author.

No. 3 . . . Illustrations, Patterns, and the front cover beadwork — Indian warrior on painted horse — was done by Author. In Volume 2, I show a purse done by Edgar Jackson of the same horse and rider. It inspired me to do one for myself. It may be fun to compare the two. In the clouds of mine, I have added in crystal beads an eagle, buffalo and bear.

No. 4 . . . The person who originally inspired me to do this series was my Navajo adopted mother Heneretta Bedonie, of Flagstaff, Az. I can find no words to express my gratitude and love for this wonderful traditional Native American Indian Lady.

No. 5 . . . To my husband, Richard Henry, who is also the publisher and made it possible. Thanks for believing in a traditional idea.

No. 6 . . . The patterns and designs shown in this volume are not all new designs. Some are transposed from pieces of beadwork and some handed down for generations — origin unknown.

No. 7 . . . A young man named Mark allowed me to photograph his beautiful cabochon beaded jewelry in Tucson, Az., two years ago. I have shown some of Mark's work in this volume. I apologize to Mark for misplacing his address, and I thank him for sharing his wonderful beadwork with us.

No. 8 . . . Thanks to hundreds of beaders that have called or written to me expressing their appreciation for this series of books and for their suggestions of topics.

About the Author

Since beginning this series of books, about two years ago, I have had very little time to do a lot of beadwork myself. As a result, I have become acquainted with beaders who have helped a great deal by submitting color slides of their own designs and similar techniques. Now there is a network of beaders in communication with each other, exchanging ideas, beads and designs, and where to purchase materials, etc. I invite anyone who does beadwork to join in. Mail a self-addressed envelope to the publisher's address on the back of the book and request the source list of catalog stores that carry beading supplies. It will be mailed to you as a compliment of the author. If you wish to submit color slides of your beadwork, they can be mailed to the same address. I can't guarantee the return of your slides. Once they are in the publisher's file, you must consider them his. If they are published in one of our volumes you will get the recognition.

For the benefit of those who haven't acquired Volumes One and Two of this series of books, I will tell a little of my background.

The last half of my professional life has been spent making my living as a designer of leather and fur garments, specializing in Native American Indian attire, which includes all types of beadwork.

I have sewn for some of the major country western stars. I have researched and done costumes for screen. I have been semi-retired for seven years now and try to concentrate my efforts on this series of teaching books concerning Native American Indian Media.

I am Native American of the Seneca Nation and admit without any reserve that GOD has blessed me in allowing me to have such a wonderful heritage. I share with you in this series of books some of my blessing.

My analogy with the ancestors of the Seneca Nation differs only with time, not in nature. It pleases me to keep alive a part of the culture of the Native American Indian, although I no longer believe in some of the religious ways of the Indian because I am a born-again Christian. I still respect their belief and admire their present-day culture as well as the past.

If we could go back in time, I would like to take you to a place of enchanted existence and acquaint you with the Native American Indian about three hundred years ago — a time when the wilderness was still wild and the rivers uncharted and in its mist, the Indian tribes of America.

Sometimes we of this push-button age think living with nature three centuries ago was a great hardship. Actually in this land of plenty there was little starvation, and all the new diseases beyond the reach of cure didn't exist. It seems to me there is a lesson to be learned from the past. If we apply the knowledge of those lifestyles to the existing, we might overcome a lot of the hardships of this modern age.

I make no claim to living as a naturalist, because I am a push-button person in my extremely modern home with hot and cold running door knobs (an old Indian friend of mine referred to my kitchen faucets as such). I am old enough to recall the trend of this world changing to a push-button existence. I call that change the plastic age, so I enjoy being able to recreate something very beautiful that isn't plastic from an age gone by. Beadwork.

This photograph was taken during Fan Fair in Nashville, Tenn. From left to right are Loddella Johnson, (the Author is wearing white squaw dress) Peggy Sue Henry, Loretta and Kay Johnson. The costumes worn by the Johnson sisters and Author were created and designed by the Author.

Materials

ou will need the following materials for doing beadwork:

#1. Beading Needles;

It would be a mistake to buy regular needles for beading. Very few if any will fit through a size eleven or smaller bead. You need the flexibility of a good thin beading needle. Most well stocked craft stores carry beading needles. You will also need Glover's or leather needles in small sizes.

#2. Thread;

Always use thread designed for beading; never a cotton thread. Cotton thread has no elasticity and frays. It will break under stress of normal use. I use Nymo Nylon for most of my projects. It comes in several weights from size A for the smallest bead to size D for the largest seed bead or to string the Warp threads on the loom.

If you are using a larger seed bead and you want a waxed thread, you can split the commercial waxed sinew like embroidery thread several times, but if you are using nylon thread you can pull the thread through BEE'S wax for any size bead.

#3. Pliers;

You will need a small pair of needle nose pliers for breaking out beads if you should end up with too many beads on a stitch or breaking out a bad bead after sewing it down. I have given an illustration on the proper way to break out a bead.

#4. Scissors;

I use a pair of small pointed man-

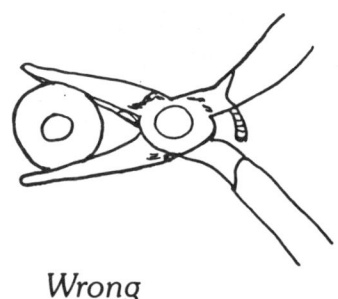

Wrong

Illustration of Incorrect and Correct way to break a bead

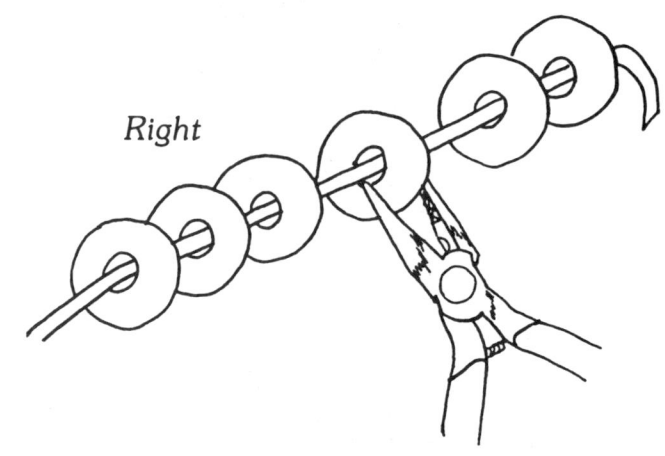

Right

icure scissors for cutting threads and trimming frayed sinew. I like the Revlon long shank manicure scissors for better control.

#5. Beading loom;

There has been only one type of loom I have used for the past twenty-five years, and that is the one illustrated in each volume of Beads to Buckskins. It is lightweight, weighing only about three pounds, and adjusts from thirty-six inches long to as short as you wish, and you can bead six inches wide. In Volume #1, I have given the illustrated measurements for constructing your own, but if you find it too difficult you may order it by getting in touch with the publisher, whose address is on the back of the book.

There are other commercial looms available, and if you will include a self-addressed envelope the publisher will be happy to send you a list of catalog stores that carry looms and beading supplies.

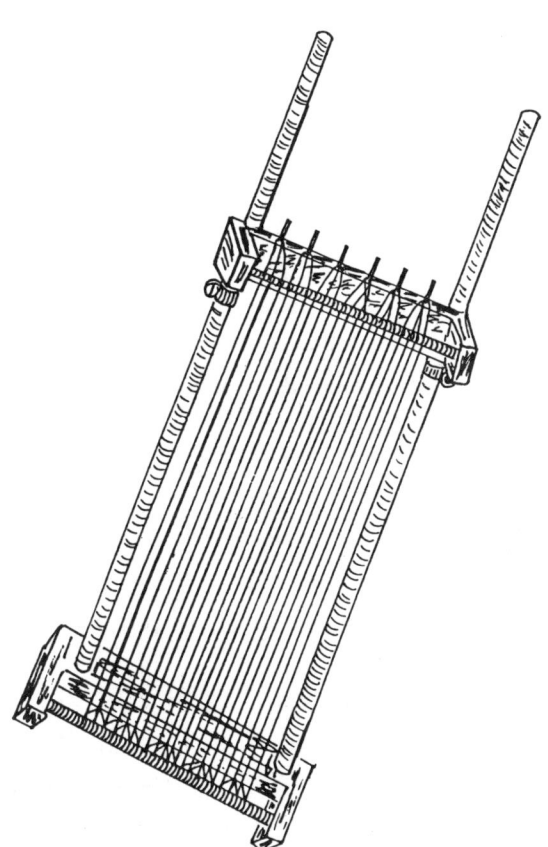

Illustration of Wooden Loom

#6. Glue and a Clear Nail Polish;

You will need a soft glue for gluing patterns to leather or several other uses described in the books. I use a leather glue which can be purchased at any store that carries leather supplies. Check the yellow pages of your phone directory. I also use super glue on certain hair barrettes and hair pieces. After I finish the barrette I like to put a very small dab of super glue at each end of the barrette to be sure the warp threads don't work out.

Clear nail polish is used to keep the end of your thread from fraying while threading the needle and dabbing a bit on knots to keep them tight.

#7. Beads;

Now let's get to the most important and fun part of your project. Choosing the correct beads.

If you are a beginner I suggest you start with a size eleven-o or size twelve-o bead. Any smaller would be difficult to see and understand what steps to take next.

If you wear glasses you might want to start with a larger bead, perhaps a size ten-o, but don't buy too many. I'm sure that as soon as you understand the fundamentals, you will want to go to a smaller bead.

There are so many different shades, cuts and sizes of beads to choose from, it can be very confusing at first. When I begin a pattern, I first color it in with felt tip highlighter pens; or regular color crayons will do. Once you have finished the color fill-in, take the pattern with you to the bead store and buy as close to the colors you have colored in, and if you cannot match the color of your choice then choose your second choice of color right then. Buy all the beads you will need for that project at the same time. If you try to match them later, it will be difficult if the store is out and has to order them.

Beads are like yarn. The shades can be different with each lot. If possible, buy beads that are all made by the same company and at the same time. A lot of stores only buy from one bead company.

The cut beads are a lot more expensive than most other beads; therefore, I sometimes use them only for highlighting. When I'm making a piece to be sold, I use standard beads because of the cost. It is difficult to sell a piece and get the price necessary to cover the cost of cut beads and the labor involved.

The Japanese Hexagon cut beads are fun to work with and are available in at least twenty-seven colors and shades. Some are lusters and some are metallic; all are opaque and small in size. I haven't discovered any of that particular bead in translucent glass as yet.

Usually the size thirteen needles will fit through most beads up to size eleven, sometimes twelve if you don't use double thread. Size B thread will work for those sizes also. Any smaller bead size and you must go to a smaller needle and thread. Size thirteen and fourteen beads take a size A thread, and I use size fifteen needles made by a company in England, "Best Quality." For size sixteen, eighteen or smaller beads I use the S. Thomas & Son needle, size sixteen with a size A or 000 thread.

Keep you bead sizes sorted to the same size and colors separated. If possible, I work out of the same container that I store my beads in. I find that the clear plastic fly-tying containers that screw together in a stack of five or six works well for both storing and working out of. The beads are easily recognizable for color. All you have to label is the size.

It's so easy to get the bead sizes mixed up, so I suggest for the beginner that you buy only one size bead until you familiarize yourself with the fundamentals of beading.

The beaded earrings are so versatile. Many different styles of beads can be used together without too much difficulty. The bugle bead is used a lot as the anchor row and in fringe. Sometimes you can get away with using different sized beads in hanging fringe, but it's wise not to try it in loom work or applique. In the color pages I have shown earrings that have stone beads in combination with glass seed beads, and it makes a very becoming piece of jewelry.

Try to cull out the bad beads or misformed ones before you start your project. If you are doing applique, fill the bead up with thread even if you have to double the thread. This keeps the bead from turning and makes for a tighter finish.

I have prepared a list of stores that have a catalog for beading supplies. If you will mail a self-addressed envelope to the publisher's address on the back of the book requesting this information, you will receive it within six weeks.

Brief Review on Loom Beading

To avoid taking a lot of pages to cover a technique that has been extensively illustrated and instructed in volumes one and two of this series of books, I will only briefly go over the basics of loom beading. This includes stringing the loom and how to begin and end the loomed weave.

There is one simple version of loom beading illustrated in this chapter that is very seldom used, but it should be applied to a lot of the beaded necklaces to avoid discomfort around the back of the neck.

Usually when these beautiful necklaces are finished off, there remains at the back of the necklace a tassel of fringed beads or a ridge marking the connection of the two loomed strips. To avoid these cases, adjust your loom for a longer piece of beadwork and bead a strip long enough to go around the back of the neck, extending from the front in the collarbone area around to the other side (usually twelve to fourteen inches). If you want a narrower strip or a progressively narrowing strip, use fewer beads in graduated steps toward the back of the neck and add beads as you approach the other side. Be sure to measure the rows or count the beads to make the sides proportionate.

The next step is to string the neckline beads that reach to the next loomed neckline piece. They will be strung on the end strings, or warp, that have been tied around the nails at the top of the loom. If these strings are shorter than you need them to be, tie an additional length of thread to the warp with a very small knot, put a dab of clear nail polish on it and allow to dry completely. Then thread your needle and string the warp thread with the neckline beads, covering the knot with a bead.

I lay my loomed beadwork on a piece of carpet sample after I have cut it loose from the loom, too keep it from slipping around while connecting the warp threads.

Unless you are an experienced loom beader, I suggest you refer to volume one or two of Beads to Buckskins books for more detailed instruction.

The loom illustrated extends to thirty-six inches and will accommodate work up to six inches wide. It can be purchased through the publisher's address on the back of this book. Send a self-addressed stamped envelope for information.

It will take a loom equivalent to this size to loom the necklaces shown in the color pages in this volume and in volume two. The illustrated directions for constructing this loom are provided in volume one of this series. You will want to read the secrets revealed in the pages of volume two as well; it will save you a lot of time with other beaded projects.

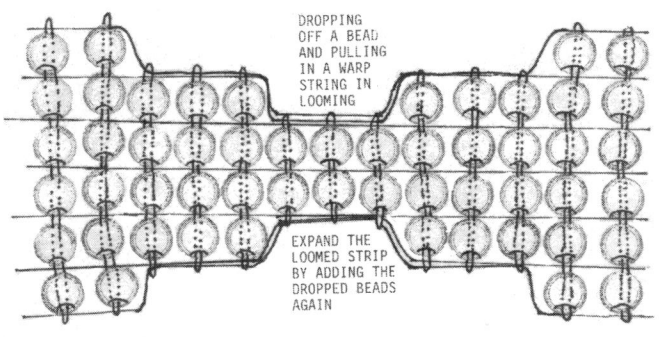
DROPPING OFF A BEAD AND PULLING IN A WARP STRING IN LOOMING

EXPAND THE LOOMED STRIP BY ADDING THE DROPPED BEADS AGAIN

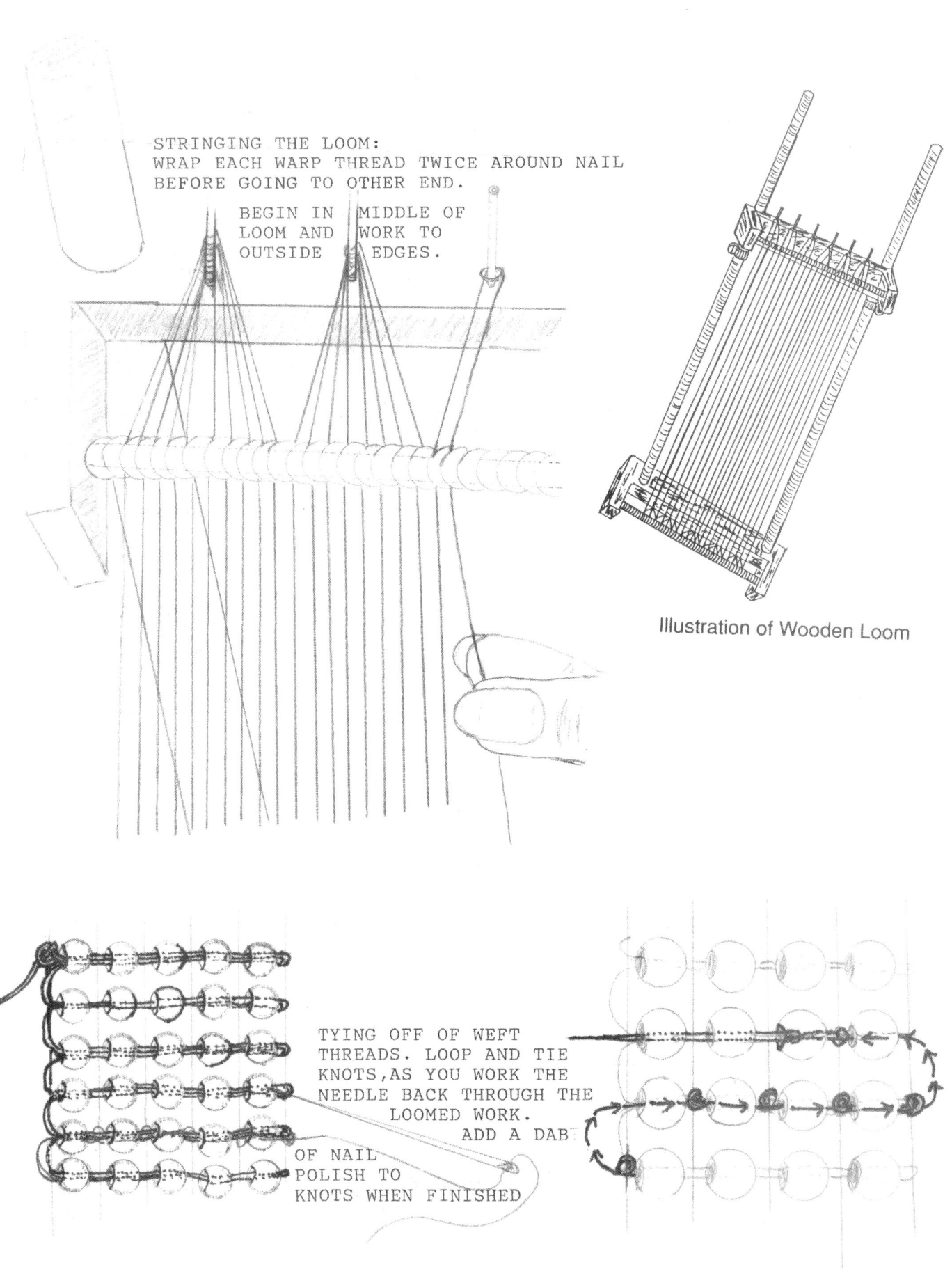

Illustration of Wooden Loom

STRINGING THE LOOM:
WRAP EACH WARP THREAD TWICE AROUND NAIL BEFORE GOING TO OTHER END.

BEGIN IN MIDDLE OF LOOM AND WORK TO OUTSIDE EDGES.

TYING OFF OF WEFT THREADS. LOOP AND TIE KNOTS, AS YOU WORK THE NEEDLE BACK THROUGH THE LOOMED WORK.
ADD A DAB OF NAIL POLISH TO KNOTS WHEN FINISHED

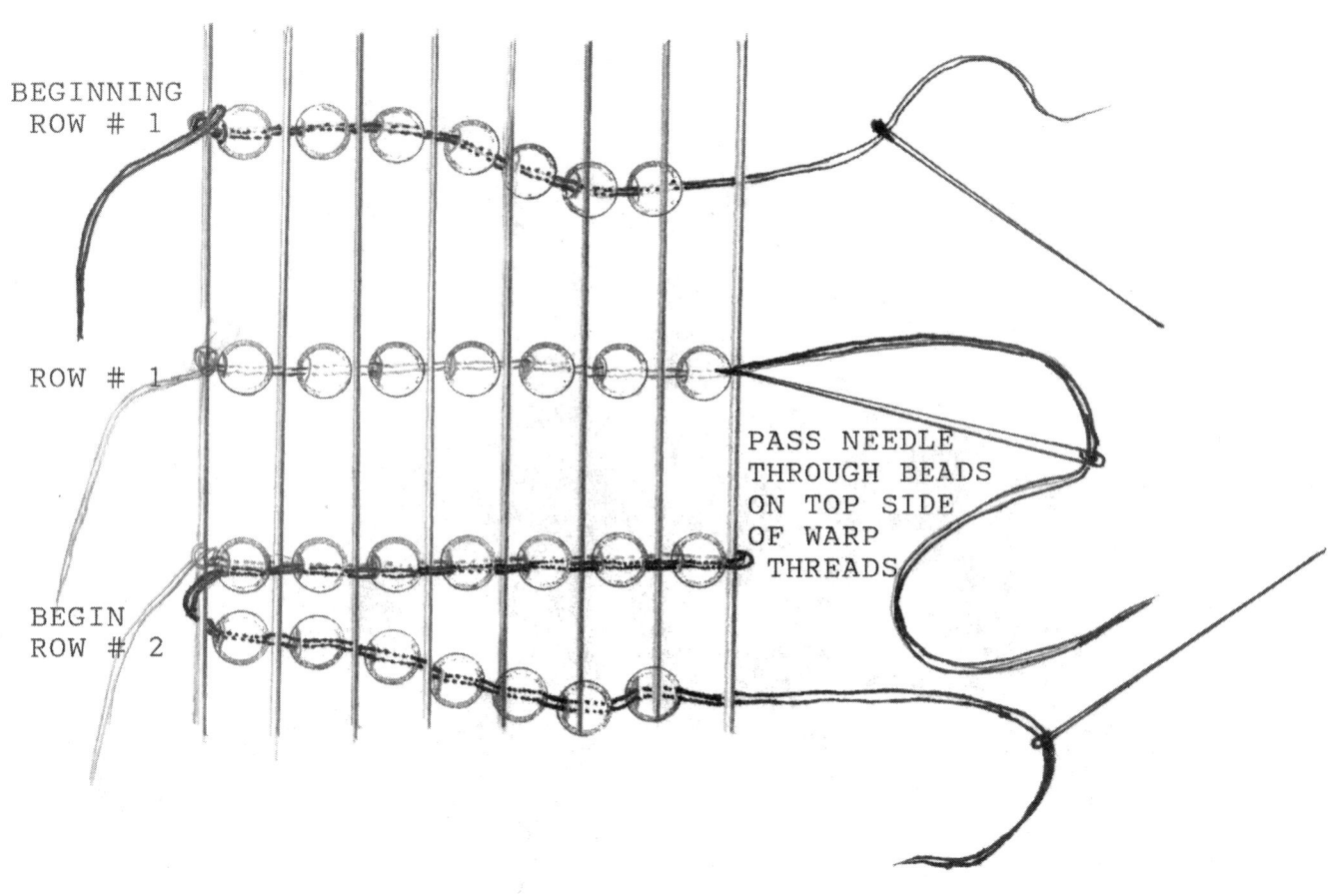

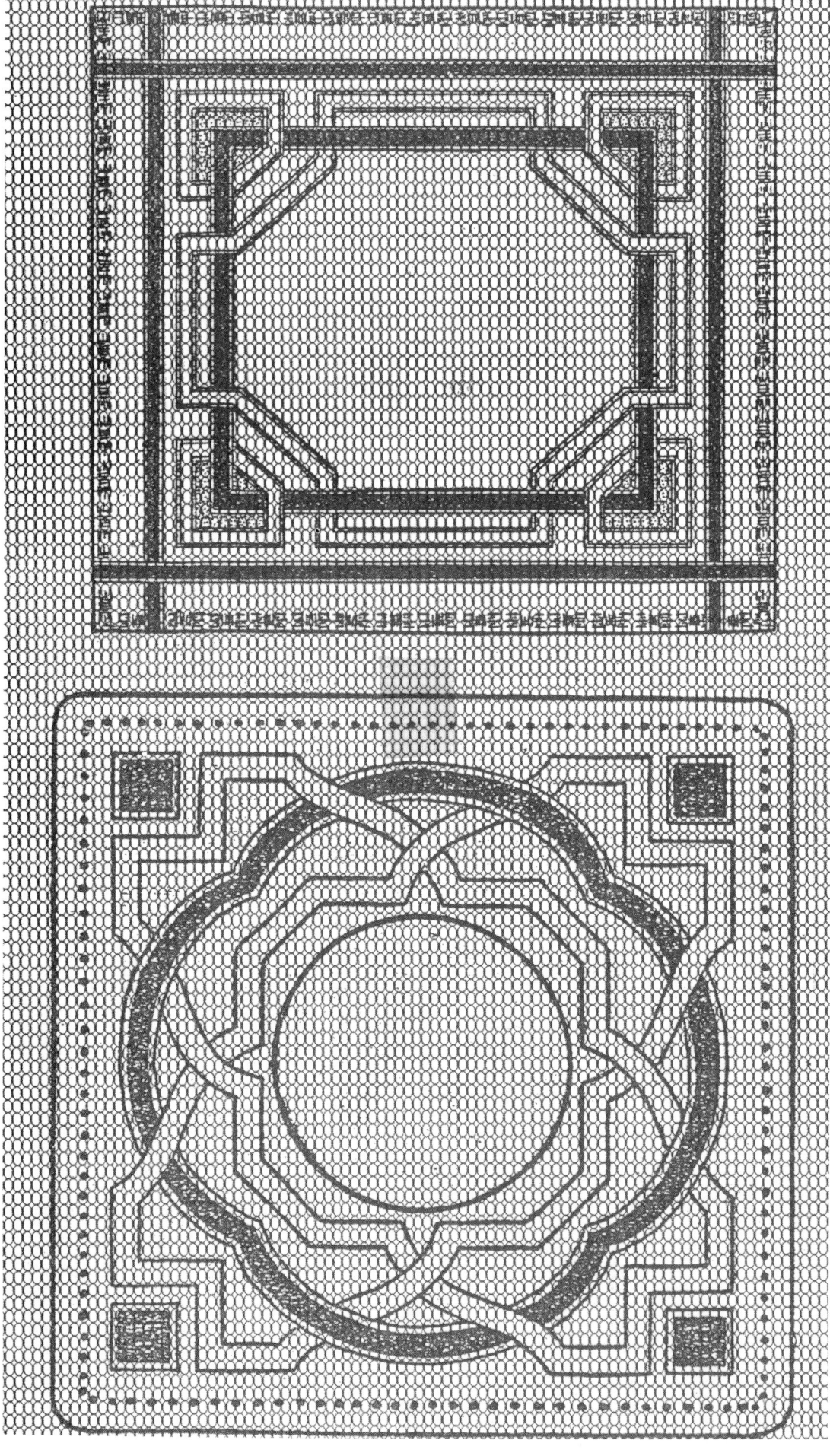

The patterns on this page and the following page are very old leather tooling patterns laid across them and photographed. The transparent graph paper is wonderful to work with. You can bead almost any picture simply by laying the graph paper over and taping in place to prevent it from moving while you are beading it. If you are interested in knowing more about the transparent graph paper, send a self-addressed envelope to the pulisher's address requesting information about it.

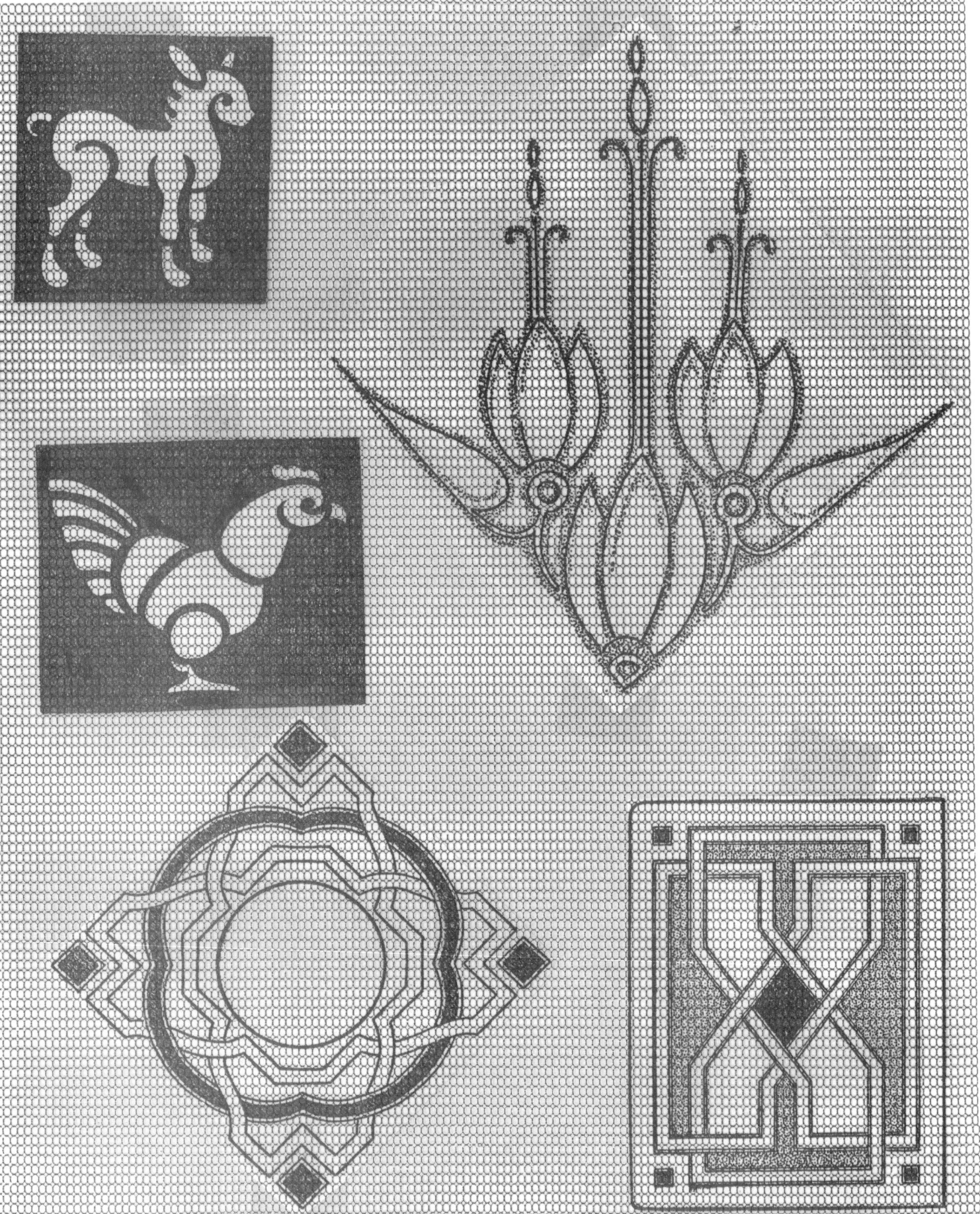

*"The End of Trails"
on graph.
Requested by many readers*

The Elusive Technique of the Peyote Stitch

In volume two I promised you more extensive coverage of the Peyote stitch as well as easy illustrations. In keeping with my promise, I will show you the traditional method and a simplified version. (Actually the simplified version has been illustrated in volumes one and two of Beads to Buckskins.)

Because the finished appearance of this weave is so complex, beaders who have never tried it think it is too time-consuming and difficult. We can dispel that myth right now: the Peyote stitch is really very simple when you understand the basics.

There are two illustrations given, allowing you to choose between the traditional and the simplified technique.

To begin with, you don't have to start with an odd number of beads unless the pattern you are using calls for it. Almost any pattern can be done with this weave. Traditionally, the Peyote stitch has been used for beading round or curved objects because of its versatility and stability. It weaves as tightly or loosely as necessary and can be used on flat objects also. The earlier traditional method was frequently used on the feathers of the headdress and around necklace strings, pipes, bows, or any round object that needed special decoration.

I use it for earrings, especially the porcupine quill earring that calls for a round beaded cylinder at the top.

It's easy to get a spiral pattern going with the Peyote stitch. First, attach or tie the anchor (top) row. This is row number one in the illustration of the simplified version. (We will get to the traditional method next.) After attaching the first row bring your needle through the last bead of the first row and begin the second row. When you have completed the second row bring your needle back through the last bead and start the third row (see illustration #3, simplified version). Continue each row in the same manner until the pattern is complete.

For me, the above method is a lot easier to do and looks a little neater than the traditional version, as the longer stitches in the traditional sometimes give rise to long lengths of string showing through the beads. Nevertheless, I will explain the three drop Peyote stitch to you. Step-by-step illustrations are included.

The beads cover a cylinder in the illustration. Begin first or top row: To make an even pattern, begin with a number of beads that can be divided evenly by six. Be sure you have enough beads to go around the cylinder—then remove one-third of the beads and space them evenly around the cylinder after tying a knot, or when you have determined how many beads you will need for the first row. You can sew them on, spaced evenly, as illustrated in Step One of the Traditional Three Drop Peyote Technique.

After getting the first row in place (snug and tight), bring your needle back through the last bead of the first row.

Second row: Pick up one bead on your needle. Bring the needle through the third bead of the first row. Pick up another bead and go through the fifth bead of the first row. Continue around the cylinder, attaching a bead to every other bead in the first row until the second row is complete.

Third and subsequent rows: Bring your needle through the first bead of the second row, pick up a bead and go through the second bead of the second row. You are now in a position to continue around and around the cylinder for as long as is necessary to complete your project. I have illustrated the start of the second row in Step Two.

If you have a problem, just study the illustration carefully and compare with your pattern. I'm sure it will come easily to you if you don't rush through the instructions.

If you are still having a problem after having looked everything over carefully, I suggest the following:

Gather these materials:

1. The paper cone center from a roll of toilet tissue or paper towels.

2. Three different colors of pony or crow beads.

3. A few yards of heavy thread or waxed sinew.

Practice the peyote stitch around the large paper cylinder, using a different color pony bead for each row. You will not need a needle if you use the waxed sinew and it will be easier for you to see your mistakes and correct them. This is not intended to be a permanent piece of beadwork—make your practice work look like the one in the illustration.

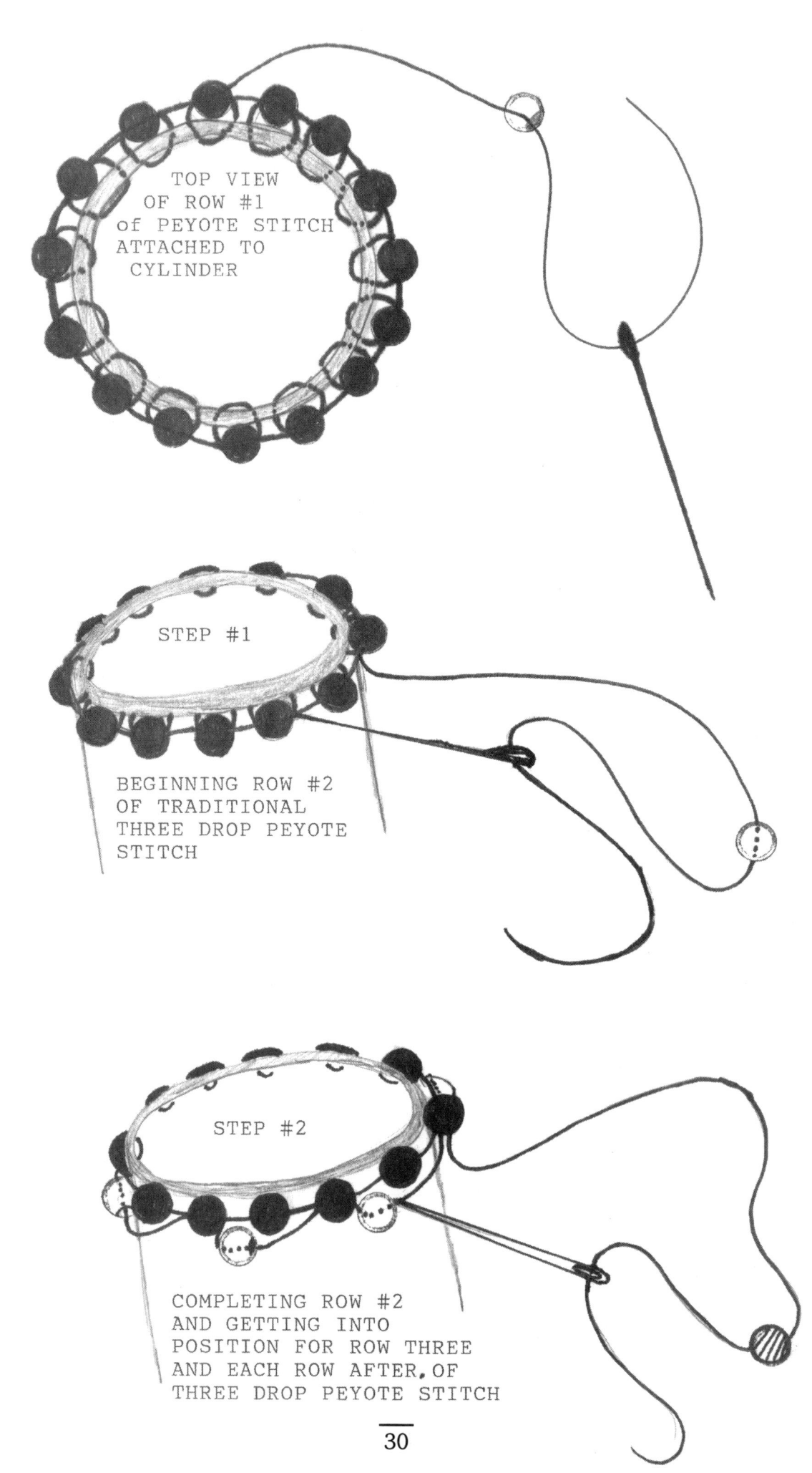

BELOW: Illustrated rows; #1, #2, #3 of the traditional three three drop PEYOTE STITCH.

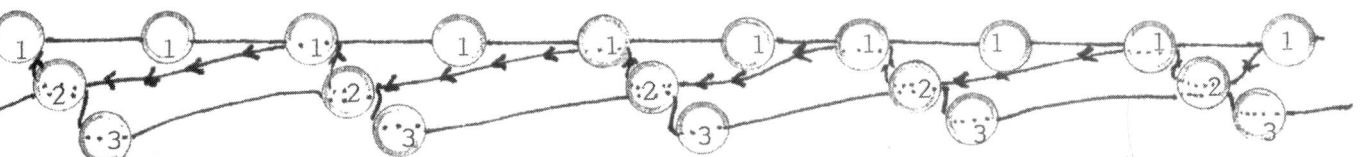

STEP #1- BELOW: ROW ONE OF THE SIMPLIFIED VERSION OF PEYOTE TECHNIQUE

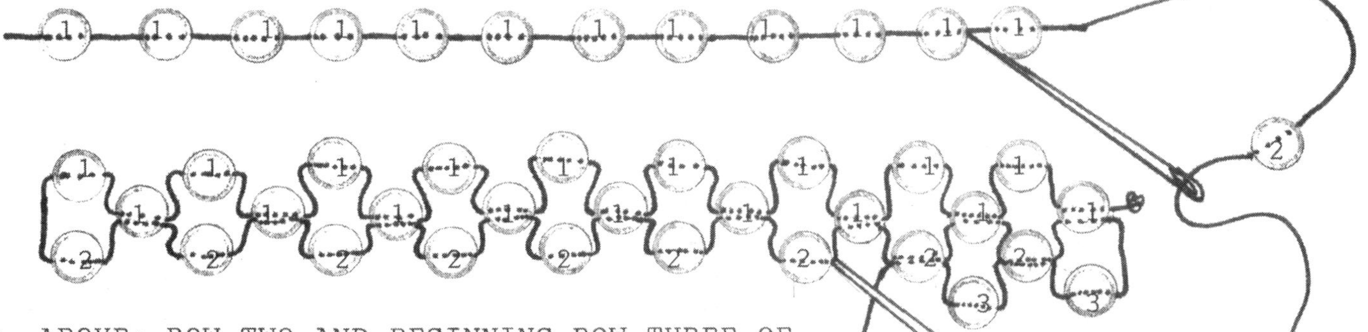

STEP #2- ABOVE: ROW TWO AND BEGINNING ROW THREE OF SIMPLIFIED VERSION OF PEYOTE STITCH

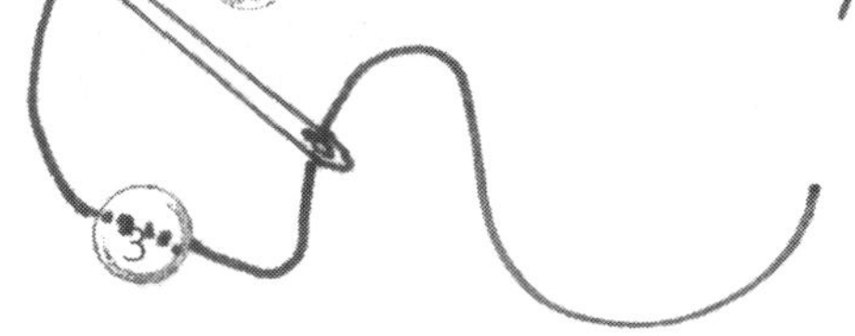

CLOSE UP OF SIMPLIFIED VERSION ON CYLINDER ROW ONE AND FINISHING ROW TWO →

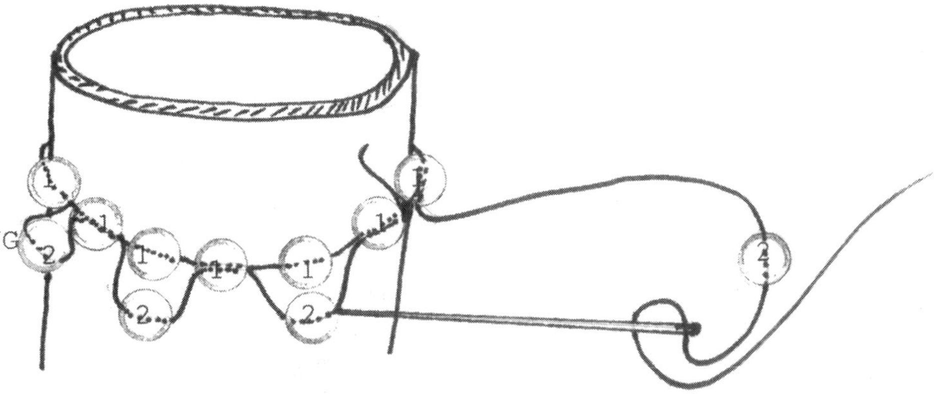

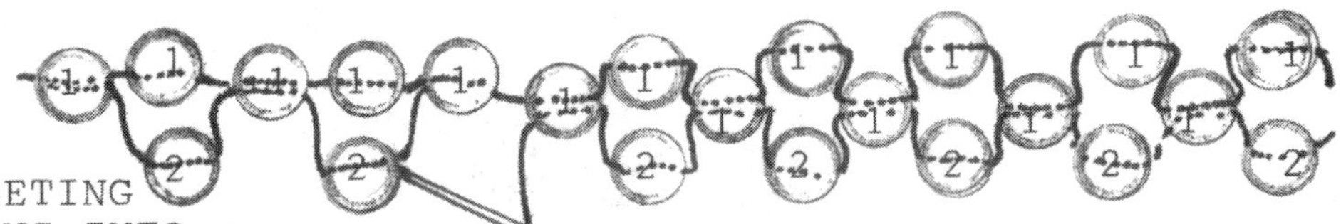

CLOSE UP OF COMPLETING ROW TWO AND GETTING INTO POSITION FOR ROW THREE OF SIMPLIFIED VERSION ON CYLINDER

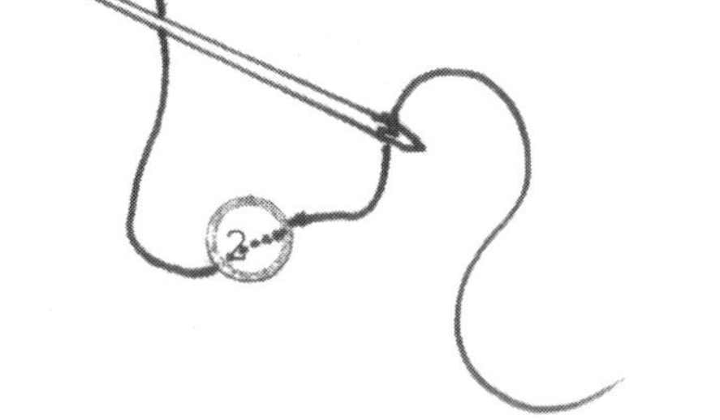

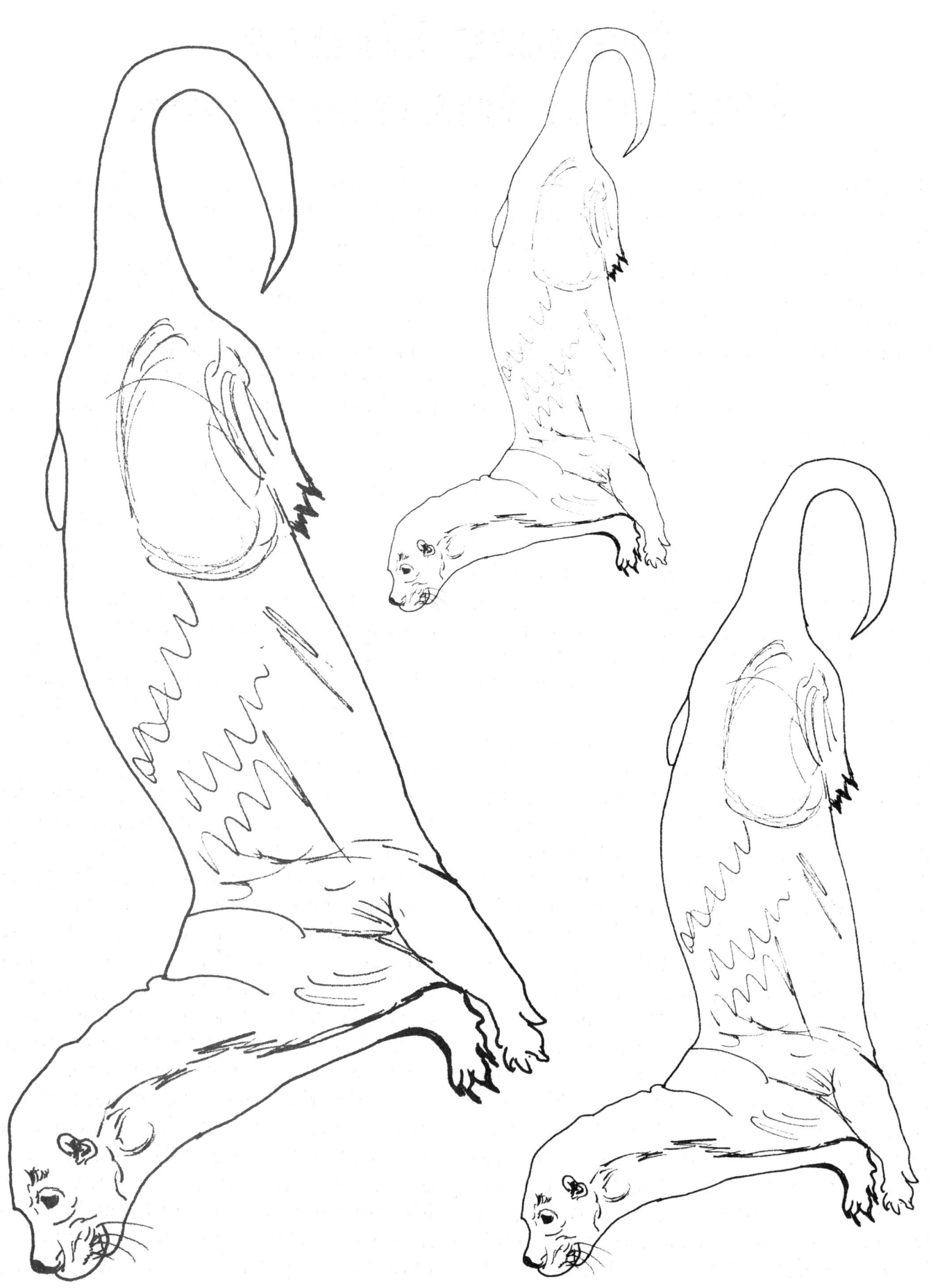

Squaw Dress Pattern Instructions

This squaw dress pattern is very easy to assemble. It will take three large deer skins for a dress size sixteen or under. For a larger size you will need enough deer skin to make inserts on each side of the dress, the length of the dress. To put the inserts in, you will have to lace two seams on each side of the dress instead of one. Use the flat stitch illustrated.

Remember that buckskin stretches. The hide will stretch more from side to side than from head to tail. If your buckskin is professionally tanned you can take a lot of the stretch out by wetting and stretching the hide before you begin your garment. Stretching first prevents a lot of sagging and bagging later, so in the long run it is worth the effort.

To begin the stretching process, hang an old sheet or five- or six-foot piece of clean cloth on a fence or a wall of your garage. A piece of plywood will do if you don't have a wall available. Next, submerge the buckskin in a tub of warm water. Then hang over a clean clothesline until all the water has stopped dripping from the skin.

While the leather is still damp but not dripping tack it to the wall, through the sheet, hair side (or top grain) out. Start tacking at the bottom, about one inch from the edge of the hide. You may need to tack the top out of the way temporarily; don't drive the temporary tacks in very far. After you have tacked across the bottom, three or four inches apart, stretch one side and tack as you stretch. Then do the other side. Remove the temporary tacks from the top and stretch the top as far as you can, tacking as you stretch.

Protect the hide from hot sun as much as possible, and allow it to dry completely. The leather will dry softer if you hang another sheet over it, to keep it from drying too quickly. Usually, once the dress is made, the leather will soften somewhat, but after it is worn a couple of times it will conform to the body's shape and soften still further.

If you are a seamstress, and have a dress form in your size, you can dampen the dress again, put it on the form. The dress will conform to your body's measurements as it dries.

Now to create the squaw dress: Choose the best of the three hides for the top of the dress. Fold in half from the head to the tail, as illustrated. Cut an eight- or nine-inch slit along the fold in the very center of the hide, depending on your neck measurement. In other words, if your neck is sixteen inches around, cut a slit eight inches long, four inches each way from the center.

After you have cut the slit, trim it out as shown in the illustration. Then make a five-inch cut, starting from the neck slit, down the center front of the hide. Trim points off to make a rounded neckline, as shown in the illustration.

You now have the top and sleeves of your dress cut out. With the two remaining hides, make the body of the dress from the yoke line downward. Measure yourself around the bust line, add three inches and divide in half. For example, if your bust measures thirty-seven inches, adding three makes it forty, and divided in half is twenty inches. Measure your hips and make the same calculations (add three inches and divide in half).

If your hip measurement is larger than the bust measurement, then cut the side seam at an angle, as illustrated. Cut the back and the front the same, leaving the rough edge at the bottom.

Using the half measurements of your bustline and hips. The bustline measurement across the front of the dress is directly under the arms. Inset the arm holes two inches, making the yoke line four inches smaller than the bust.

To attach the body of the dress to the yoke: on the inside of the top front, draw a line with a tracing wheel (no ink or pencil) across the yoke, centered and two inches below the five-inch V-neckline cut. If you turn the top inside out and lay it flat on a table, it will be easy to work on.

After you have drawn the horizontal yoke line, which should be the same size as the cut line of the yoke on the dress body, spread leather glue or rubber cement evenly along the traced yoke line. Repeat the procedure with the yoke line on the dress body. Remember, you are making a flat seam, so when you spread the glue on the body yoke line, the glue should be on the top grain side of the leather. Then turn the dress body over and stick the two glued lines together. Press firmly with your fingers, then tap lightly along the glued seam with a small piece of wood. Don't start the back of the dress until you have completed the front.

After the glue has dried, punch a pattern of holes along the glued seam. I have illustrated the herringbone stitch and the flat stitch. It will take two lines of holes, one line on each side of the seam, punched directly across the seam, in perfect alignment. The holes should be punched one-third to one-half inch apart, depending on your choice of stitch size. Be sure the hole pattern covers the seam.

Either of the illustrated lacing stitches will be very becoming. I suggest you use the flat stitch on the side seams for comfort. When you attach the side seams, lap the front over the back seam as you glue. Leave a few inches open at the bottom for freedom of leg movement.

Fringe is optional, but traditionally the legs of the animal are fringed, which translates to the area hanging longer on the insides of the sleeves. Fringe at the bottom of the dress was worn in summer, to keep bugs away as well as for ornament.

Fringe serves many purposes: it allows the rain to drip off the garment with less penetration; it keeps the bugs away; and as you move, the fringe sways. It also represents the roots of the Native American Indian, always going down to mother earth.

STEP # 1 OF HERRINGBONE LACED STITCH

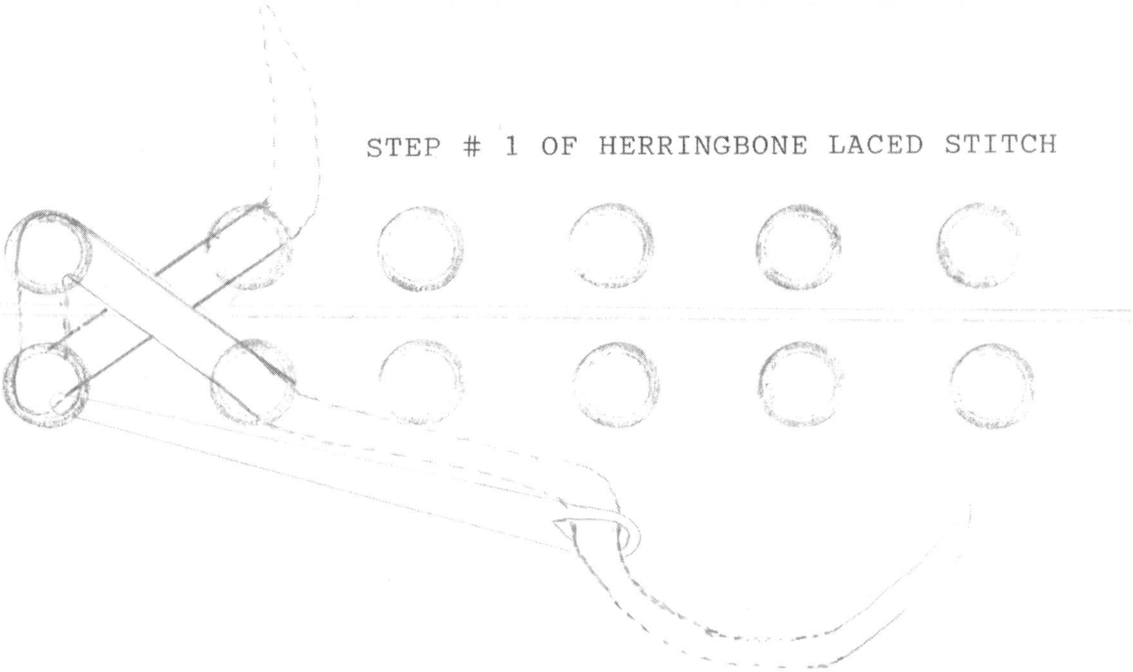

STEP # 2 OF HERRINGBONE LACED STITCH

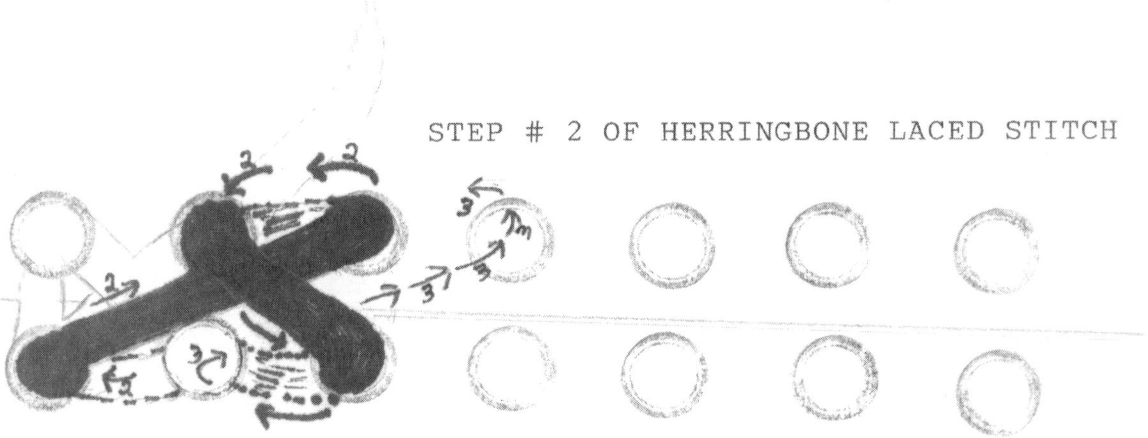

BEGINNING STEPS OF THE FLAT STITCH

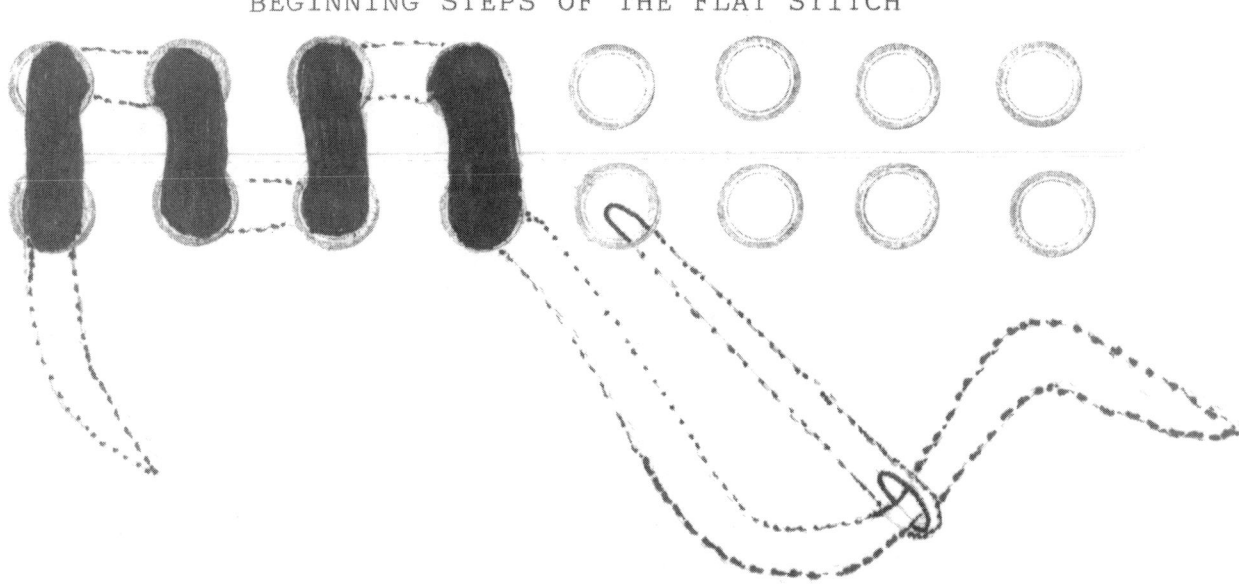

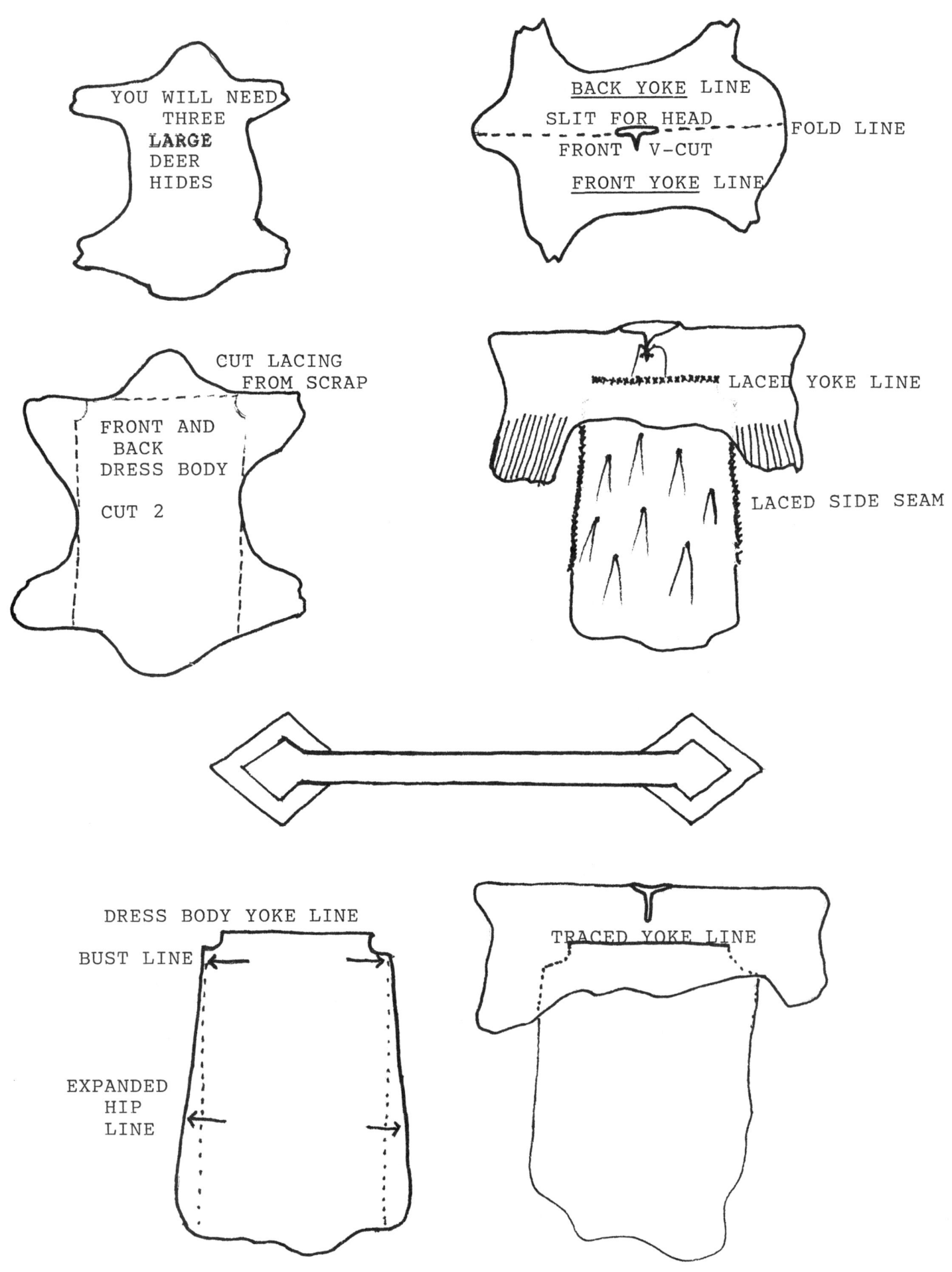

Moccasin Pattern Instructions

Wet and stretch leather, according to the directions given with the Squaw Dress instructions.

If you are going to bead your moccasins, it will be much easier if you bead them before you sew them together, while they are flat.

The moccasin is made from three pieces of leather and can be turned into a high leg wrapped moccasin easily.

Trace the outline of your foot onto a piece of paper. A brown shopping bag works well for patterns, as it is strong and quite flexible.

After tracing your foot, carefully measure 5/8-inch out from your outline and draw another outline 5/8-inch outside the first. This piece will be the sole of your moccasin (see illustration). Cut the sole pattern out and lay it on another piece of paper. Measuring 5/8-inch outward from the front part (toe area) of the moccasin, draw a curve. Draw a straight line seven inches long across the back of the pattern, 5/8-inch out from the heel, centered along the axis of the foot. Join the ends of the outlines at an angle, enclosing the entire shape, as shown. This piece is the top of the moccasin.

Make a slit from the back center toward the tongue line, two-thirds of the length of the top. Cut the tongue line, two inches long from side to side, as illustrated.

Before you start cutting the moccasins out of the leather, check your pattern and make sure everything is cut and traced exactly like the illustrations.

After you have cut one moccasin out, turn the sole over and cut the other sole out, using the first sole as a pattern.

The little arrow tabs are important. Glue and sew them into place and they will keep your moccasin from ripping. Then sew the tongue on while the moccasin is flat.

Next, sew the back seam together. It will be more comfortable if you use a flat stitch for sewing the back seam.

Now you are ready to attach the sole. Take one stitch at the toe, one at each side and at the heel, to hold the moccasin together while you are attaching the sole. Begin sewing the top and sole together at the front of the moccasin, one side at a time. If you have any stretch you can take it out at the back seam.

Next punch holes and add the lace. For extra long-wearing moccasins, cut an inner sole: Turn your moccasin inside out and glue an inner sole to the inside bottom with leather glue. Allow glue to dry completely before wearing.

MOCCASIN PATTER ILLUSTRATIONS

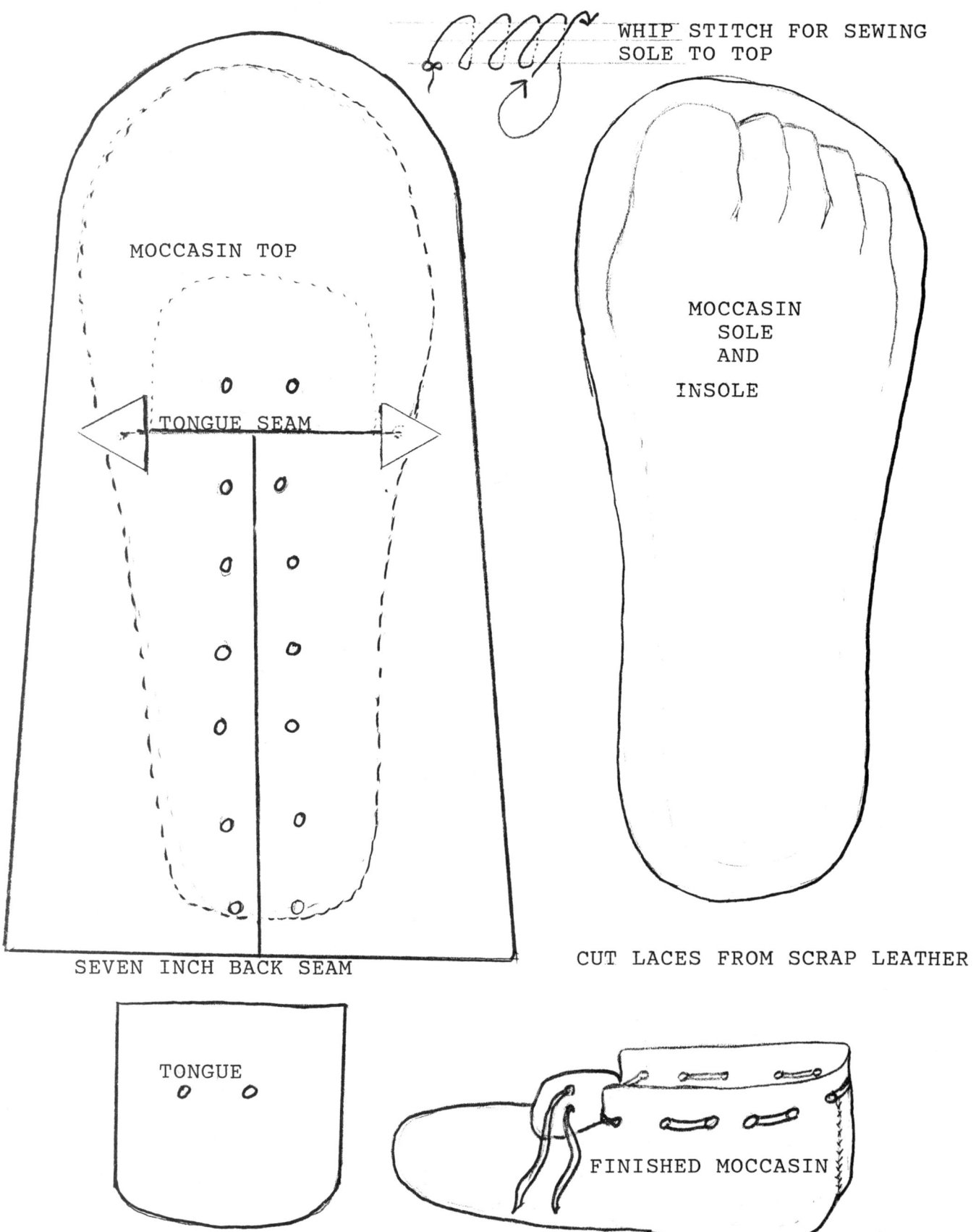

Buckskin cape trimmed in beaver fur and fringed worn over white squaw dress. Created and designed by the author.

White buckskin squaw dress designed and created by the author

Little Navajo niece of Author 'D'nello Bedonnie of Flagstaff, Az. Squaw Dress, leggins and footwear was done by Author

Pictured in white squaw dress, "Anita Carter" of the Carter Family with Author. The squaw dress and boots were created by Author.

Gold Elk skin coat with coyote collar. Hand laced pockets and yokes with extra long sleeve and yoke fringe. Created by Author.

Gold buckskin fringed coat trimmed in red fox with red fox collar. Features long, off-shoulder fringe. Author is wearing her own creation.

Gold elk, triple fringed, hand laced jacket. Elk horn buttons. Created by Author.

A black-powder dream. Badger fur fronted coat. Featuring a complete badger pelt for collar, head and tail still attached. The leather is brain-tanned buckskin. Created and designed by Author.

Ladies Gold Elk Skin with Coyote collar, and men's white buckskin coat with white wolf collar. Both feature hand laced seams and hand cut fringe. Created by Author. Models are my friends Tom and Mendy Lutz of the Hee Haw Theater, Branson, Mo.

Fully beaded Fancy Dancer. This young man from Oregon did all his own beadwork and feather bustle.

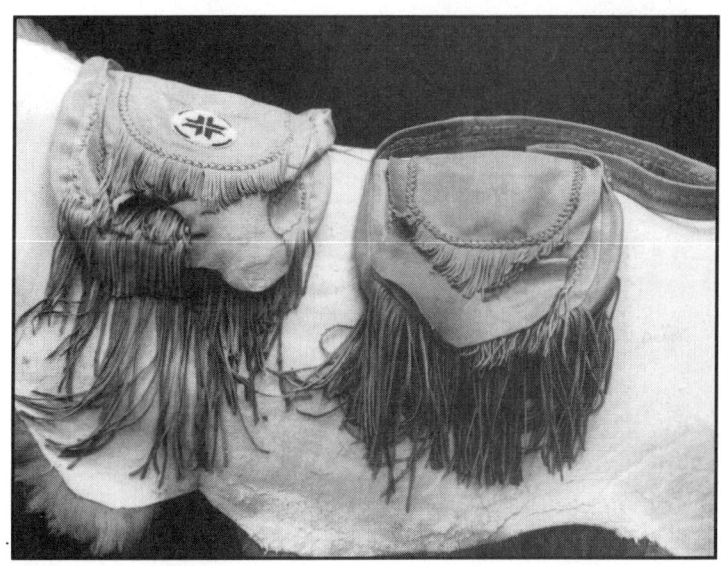

Buckskin beaded purses, Hand laced and fringed. Created by Author.

I present these photographs as a tribute to these two great entertainers who have now passed on. They were wonderful inspiring people to be around. I had the pleasure of creating garments for both of them and their families.

The top photograph is Grady Nutt in a white buckskin shirt with ermine tails. Grady was a very humorous man both on stage and off.

The bottom photograph shows Kenny Price with the Author. Kenny is wearing a white elk skin vest. Kenny was a regular on the Hee Haw Show as Grady was. Kenny was better known for his wonderful singing voice.

How To Brain Tan Deer and Elk Skins

ou can tan your own deer or elk skin the traditional Indian way but it will take a lot of hard work and patience.

The Native American Indian has used the brain tanning method for centuries. It has proved to be one of the best for withstanding the elements. To tan the skin they used the brain and tallow (fat) of the animal they killed for food, wasting nothing that could be used for their survival.

To begin the tanning process, carefully skin the animal without cutting even the smallest knife holes in the skin. A little hole can become large in size during tanning.

Flesh and wash the hide until all blood, membrane and fat have been cleaned from the skin.

The simplest way to flesh a hide is to stretch it across a peeled log, or cover a wooden sawhorse with some padding and stretch the hide, then begin scraping and trimming every inch.

After you have scraped and cleaned the flesh side of the animal, fill a large tub or container with cold clean water. Be sure you have enough water to cover the hide and then some. Next mix one cup of wood ashes with two cups of cold water. Stir it up real well, then stir the ash mixture into the tub of cold water. Place the hide in the tub of lye-ash water and let it soak in the tub until the hair begins to come out with a slight tug. Stir the contents of the tub a few times and leave the hide in the water a while longer, until you can scrape a blunt scraping tool gently across the skin a few times and remove a strip of hair. At this point you will be able to scrape all the hair off.

If you are finding it difficult to deal with the odor, you can change the lye-ash water several times, but it will slow down the hair slipping process.

When the hair has reached the slipping stage, stretch the hide across the log again, hair side up, and begin scraping the hair off.

Next, in a small pot, place the brain of the animal along with two cups of fat or tallow and simmer until you can mix it together, making a paste.

Once the paste has cooled, and you have removed all the hair from the hide, rub the brain paste into the hide, covering the entire skin and rubbing in well. Let the hide rest, soaking up the paste and becoming dry to the touch.

After the hide is has dried up all the brain paste, pull the hide across a wooden sawhorse or peeled limb of a tree to soften. When you have made it as soft as possible by pulling, then add the finished softener by scraping the hide gently with a clean sandstone.

Sometimes the Indian would smoke the hide for color as well as to preserve it. Smoking also hid their scent from larger game animals, and it was said to keep the snakes from the path. Snakes can detect the smoke. The best way to smoke the skin is with a very small green wood fire that has lots of coals. Hang the skin several feet above the fire and channel the smoke to it.

The rodeo patterns were inspired after attending a rodeo as the guest of some of the performers. Linda Scholtz and Vickie Tyler put on a dazzling display of trick riding, and their costumes were all sparkle with beads and sequins.

Paul Scholtz, Linda's husband, informed me that rodeo people appreciate good beadwork too. They are learning to do special decor in beadwork for their tack and personal costumes. These people are of a special kind. Good luck to you all.

BRONCO RIDER

TRICK RIDER

BULL RIDER

Rodeo Patterns

Rodeo Patterns

Belt Buckle Frame Suggestions

Large hand-sewn collar set in pinks and salmon. By Shalimar Tracey.

Grey clay set in a triple pointed diamond design. By Shalimar Tracey.

Mayan style bib necklace with earrings. By Shalimar Tracey.

Large double diamond necklace. By Shalimar Tracey.

Beaded Medicine Pouch. Courtesy of Green River Traders, Dubois, Wy.

Loomed Hat Bands done by Cory Kennedy of Hill City, Kansas.

Beaded Knife and Scabbard. Courtesy of Green River Traders, Dubois, Wy.

Fringed loomed necklace. Courtesy of Jude Biegert, "The Bead Lady."

Beaded rosette hair pieces. Author's.

These lovely beaded cabochon earrings were done by Jan Wordrip, of Milton Freewater, Or.

Assortment of earrings, one is the U.S.A. flag done with the brick stitch, pattern shown in Volume Two of series.

Peyote stitch-beaded pool cue. Author's

Peyote stitch beaded ink pen. Courtesy of Green River Traders, Dubois, Wy.

Loom beaded necklace. Author's

Assortment of loom beaded belts. Done by Cory Kennedy, Hill City, Ks.

Beaded turtle pouch. Author's

Split loom beaded necklace. Author's.

Assortment of beaded belt buckles done in floral and silhouettes. Author's

Apache Burden Baskets in miniature. Peyote stitch. Author's

Four appliqued belt buckles, each with a different animal. Author's.

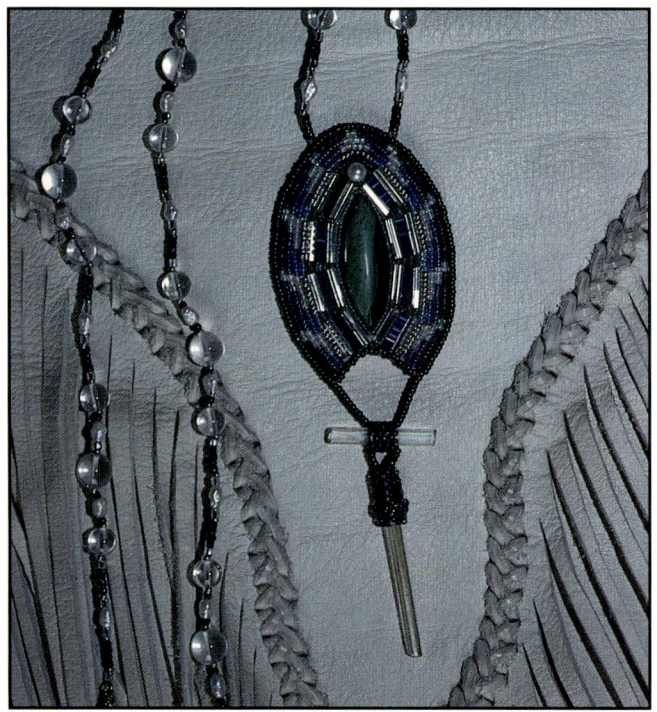

In this beautiful piece, Mark has chosen a green stone cabochon as his center piece and put a natural crystal cross at the bottom adding a crystal bead neckline.

Beaded cabochon necklace, elegantly done with size sixteen glass bead, stone cabochon, and natural crystals. Courtesy of "Jewelry by Mark," Quartzsite, Az.

This necklace features a natural crystal formation as the center theme with crystal bead for the neckline. Again the little sixteen seed bead has done its work. I tip my hat to my old friend Mark.

Mark has captured the beauty of this natural blue-green crystal formation by surrounding it with a delicate pattern of beadwork in size sixteen glass seed beads.

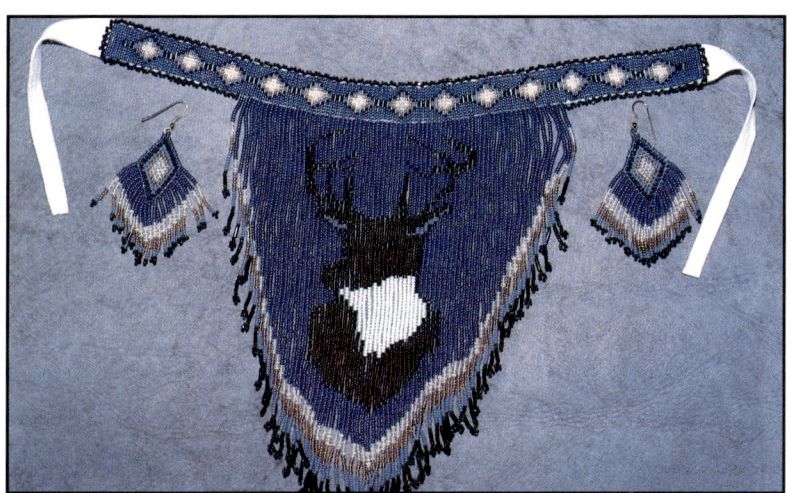

Doris arranged this deer head necklace in soft iridescent blue. This same pattern was featured on the front cover of Volume One.

These beautiful split loomed necklaces were done by my sister-in-law, Doris Kennedy of Hill City, Ks.

These striking black necklaces are elegant and can be worn with any wardrobe. Nice job, Doris.

Doris has featured the Indian pottery in both of these lovely split loomed necklaces.

Freida has done an unusually intricate pattern in her main theme of this split loomed necklace.

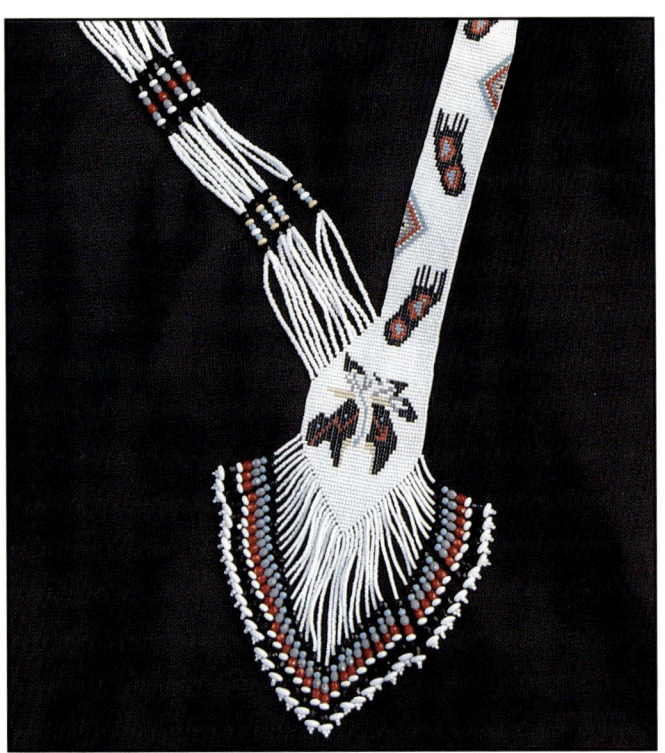

I can't say enough about Freida Bates' beadwork. She is truly a master at looming. This bear fetish necklace speaks for itself.

Again Freida has accomplished great contrast in a similar pattern as above. She has used a different neckline and choice of colors.

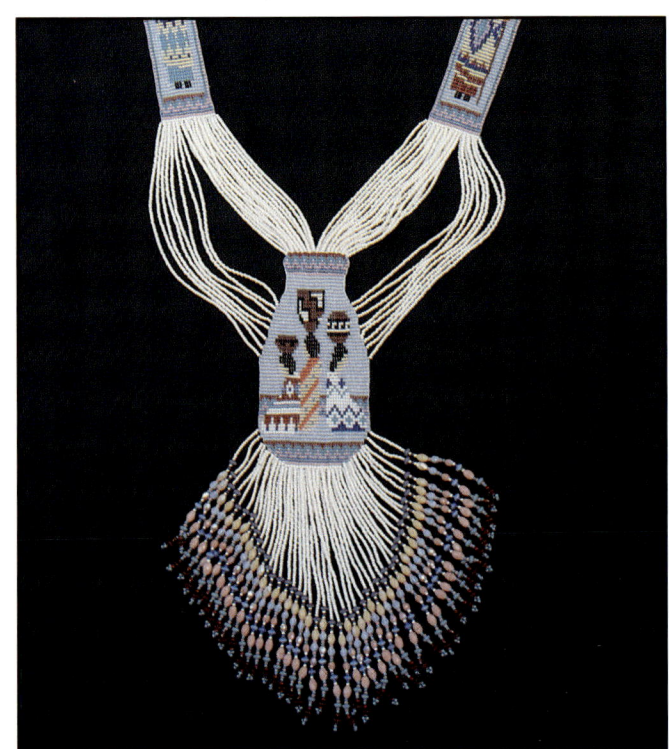

This is a very different effect Freida has achieved with this pattern.

Doves in Flight pattern for loomed necklace, or this same bird can be used for the Blue Bird design with rainbow background.

String neckline beads in repeating rainbow colors for full effect. Then do birds in shades of blue.

For this Water Bird necklace pattern, string the neckline beads on all warp strings except the center string.

For the upper water birds in the neckline, don't loom on the center string. This string is to be woven down into the main center piece after you have strung one turn bead on it.

Fringe hangs from wings and tail, beginning from the underside of the wing at the bend.

This moth pattern should be done in brown tones with splashes of teal green and beiges and a touch of soft yellow and iridescence.

This is a great pattern for the split loomed necklaces.

The small moth can be used on the neckline.

Minbre's designs, graphed from photographs of actual pieces of their pottery.

70

Beaded Cabochon Jewelry Instructions

This beautiful jewelry technique is very versatile. It can be combined with glass beads, stone beads, buttons, and even little bone elephants as Jan Wordrip has done (see color pages). You can make it as expensive or inexpensive as you choose, depending on the beads. This is an entire line of jewelry that is very popular and in demand.

When doing a special piece, I like to use a stone cabochon with two millimeter stone beads. If you have trouble finding the stone cabochons and beads, check your local Gem and Mineral society for the next gem and mineral show in your area; or drop a letter to the publisher, with a self-addressed stamped envelope, requesting the names of the companies that carry them.

In my opinion, stone beads drilled in China are the best. They seem to be more uniform and evenly drilled.

Glass seed beads also make a very beautiful piece. Antique buttons make a good center theme and are more authentic in keeping with a Native American Indian ornamental theme. The Indians incorporated buttons in a lot of their beadwork.

To make a starburst pattern around the center theme, use bugle beads. If you want a lot of detail in your pattern, use a small seed bead, size thirteen or smaller.

I'm going to start you out with an earring, then get into the larger pieces of jewelry, such as necklaces and garment ornament.

To make this earring you will need the following materials:

A lightweight piece of buckskin or beading leather, large enough to fit in an embroidery hoop six inches across (if you can't obtain leather use canvas with interfacing on the back; leather works much better for this technique); a plastic lid from a butter tub or coffee can; beading needle and thread; leather or rubber cement glue; scissors, beads and center for earrings—cabochon, button or large bead.

Step One: Draw four circles exactly the same size on the leather, the size you want for your earring. Place the leather in a small embroidery hoop.

Step Two: Glue cabochon to center of one leather circle. Make one earring at a time. When you finish the first earring up to the last circle of attached beads, then start the other one without removing the leather from the hoop.

Step Three: String as many seed beads as necessary to make a circle slightly smaller than the base of the cabochon. Arrange the seed bead circle around the cabochon. The beads should fit flush to the leather but crowned slightly over the cabochon (as illustrated: attaching Row #1). This row of beads acts to hold the cabochon on. If possible, use doubled thread through this row. As it is the anchor row, you want it to be strong.

Step Four: Row two lies flush with the leather and is attached to the anchor row (Row #1) with a Peyote stitch. (For a close-up of how the Peyote stitch is done, see the Simplified Version illustration elsewhere in this book.)

Step Five: String enough beads for the third row to circle row 2. If you are arranging a pattern in your seed beads you will need an exact count; but for your first pair I suggest using a single color for each row, or all one color.

After making your circle of beads, attach row 3 to row 2 by sewing down through the leather through the first bead. Come back through the leather and go through the second bead. Go through the next bead in row 2 and come down through the third bead in row 3. Now you are ready to go down and come up through the leather again.

I know this sounds awfully confusing, so I have illustrated how to start the first three rows. You can attach as many rows as you wish, using the same steps as for row 3, depending on how large you want your earring to be.

Step Six: After you have completed beading the circle of your earrings to the size you want, put a dab of Super Glue around row 1 next to the cabochon. Don't get carried away with the glue—a couple of drops will do the trick, and you don't want it to show. Attach the backside and center of the earring to the beaded cabochon circle. Begin by cutting two small circles out of the plastic lid, slightly smaller than the circumference of your beaded cabochon.

You must now decide if you want a post or ear wire on the earring. If you want a post, attach it by making a small hole in the plastic, offset to the top of the plastic circle (as in the illustration), and inserting the post toward the back of the earring.

Next, remove the leather from the hoop and very carefully cut out the beaded cabochon circles and the two leather circles. Take care not to cut too close to the threads. Remember to leave enough leather to sew the edge stitch on.

Glue the three disks together, using leather glue or rubber cement (not Super Glue), in the following order: With the plastic in the middle, the ear post facing toward the back, glue to the backside of the beaded cabochon circle. Then make a hole in the remaining leather circle for the ear post to go through and glue it over the plastic disk to the backside of the earring. You are making a sandwich with the plastic disk in the middle.

Allow the glue to dry, then sew around the edge with a loop stitch as illustrated.

Step Seven: Edge stitch around the earring as illustrated.

Now you are ready to add the fringe. There are many different choices of fringe, some of which are illustrated in the fringe section of this book. It is easy to design your own style. To attach the fringe, start with the center fringe and work to the outside.

The seven steps described above are the same steps to be followed when making necklaces, omitting the plastic disk and ear post.

I have illustrated a simulation of how to begin and finish a pattern using the cabochon for the central theme of a necklace. You can vary the pattern simply by changing the lines of the background pattern.

The left side of the pattern is filled in and the right side shows the lines drawn on the leather for a pattern. The fringe is optional, but I think it adds a graceful look. As for the neckline beads, those are optional too.

To begin your necklace, trace a pattern or an arrangement of lines that fit into the design you choose, onto a piece of soft buckskin or beading leather. Place the leather into an embroidery hoop and follow the step-by-step instructions and illustration for mounting the cabochon onto the leather.

After you have the cabochon mounted with three rows of surrounding beads, outline the lines of your pattern with beads using the appliqué stitch. Then fill the center of your outlined pattern.

Color is the mainstay of your design so choose beads that highlight and complement your cabochon.

Don't remove the necklace from the hoop until you are ready to cut out the completely finished pattern and glue on the leather back.

After you have cut out your finished pattern, glue it onto a piece of the remaining leather, covering up the the threads. Then trim around the edge carefully. Don't cut any threads.

I didn't show an edge stitch in the illustration, but you should do an edge stitch around the outside edge to hold the back piece of leather to the front and to cover up the leather edges.

For the neckline beads you can string single beads or use a daisy chain or chevron chain. And if you want to carry the design even further, loom a nice piece and attach it to the leather.

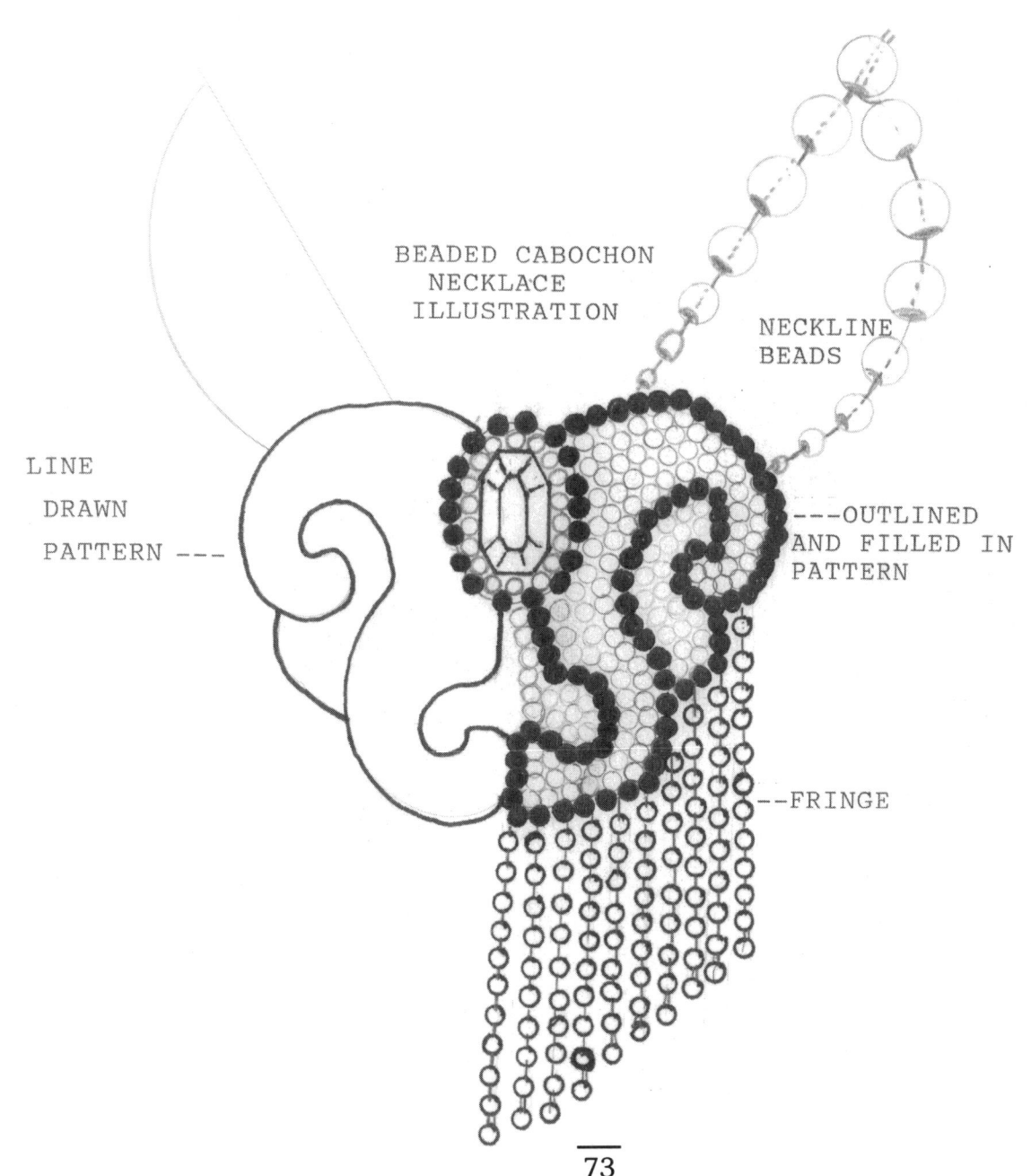

Beaded Cabochon Jewelry
Necklace & Earrings
Illustrations

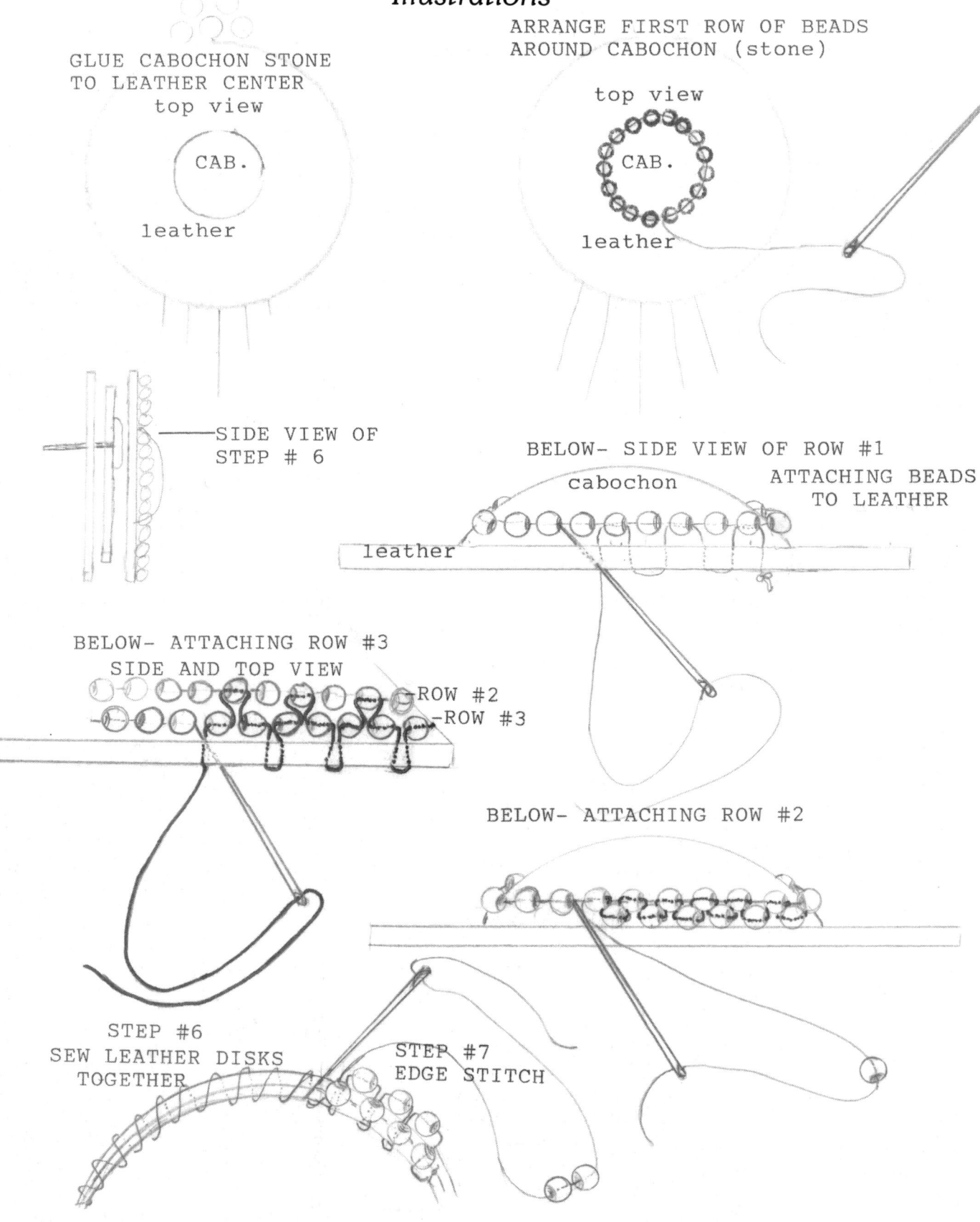

Shalimar Tracey is a very accomplished beader as you can see from the color photographs shown in the color section and also in black and white photos on this page. She has received numerous awards throughout the U.S. for her beadwork and design.

Shalimar has incorporated the brick stitch or cheyenne technique with a wide assortment of glass, stone and bone beads. Some are antique. She has a wonderful talent for combining these combinations and sizes into beautiful jewelry.

Necklace set in quadruple diamond style. It features size 13 specialty beads.
—Shalimar Tracey

Set done in heavy yellow satin bugles and melon beads. Maroon and french blue 3-x beads. Crystals are also used.
—Shalimar Tracey

Garnet double-diamond necklace set, featuring garnet drop crystals, fresh water pearls, garnet beads with over eighty triangular shaped garnets.
—Shalimar Tracey

Dark woody-rose clay and cut porcelain set. It features fresh-water pearls and cut porcelain ceramic end pieces and square beads in the neck piece.
—Shalimar Tracey

The assortment of bead work shown on this page are fun projects — fun to make and fun to wear, especially for children.

Beaded Owl belongs to Wilma Mangum of Mangum's beads, Blackfoot, Idaho. Size 16 beads were used for the medallion with larger blue beads and mother of pearl on the neck and fringe.

This little Indian is done with the peyote stitch and then attached to the medallion of feathers by his white and black head-dress. A cute technique used by the Southern California Indian.

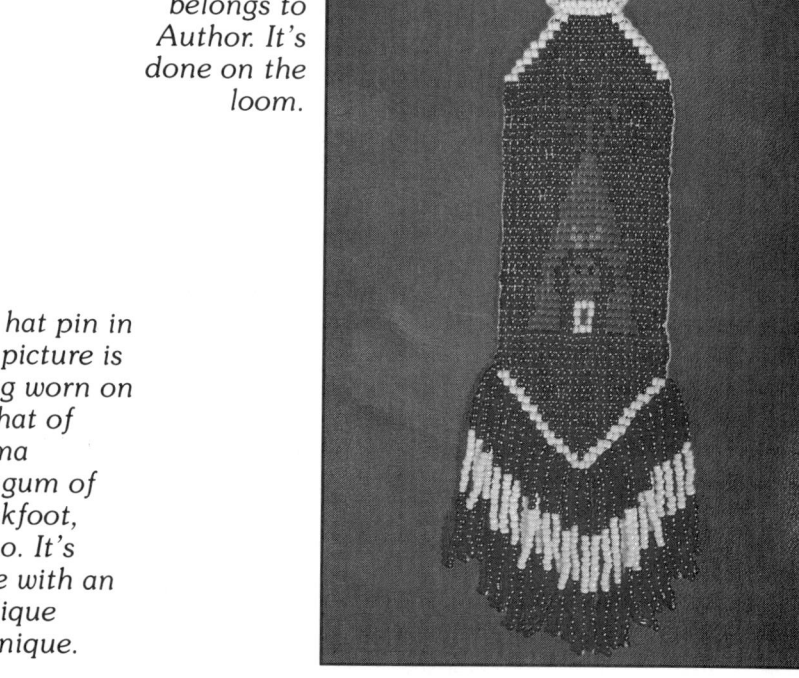

The Indian in the tee-pee (necktie) belongs to Author. It's done on the loom.

The hat pin in this picture is being worn on the hat of Wilma Mangum of Blackfoot, Idaho. It's done with an applique technique.

Loom Beading without a Loom Technique

This bead weaving technique appears to have been done on a loom, but you don't need one. While traveling across country years ago I forgot my loom at home and it was imperative that a certain piece of beadwork be done for a costume before I returned home. So I worked out this weave, riding as a passenger as my assistant drove. Since then I have used it frequently, especially in a confined area where there is no room for a large loom.

I touched on this technique briefly in volume one of this series, but not to its full extent. The simplicity of this weave is a great asset to those who do not work with the loom but would like to do the loom patterns. Actually, this technique produces a much stronger piece of beadwork than most loomed work, because each bead interlocks with the other, and each row interlocks with the rows above and below it as well as the vertical rows to each side.

Another feature of this unique little weave is that any of the beautiful loomed necklaces shown in this as well as volume two can be made with this technique. A big plus for this weave is that unlike loomed work, if you break a thread or lose a bead while wearing the finished work, you don't lose a whole row of beads, or possibly three or four, before noticing the damage.

The illustrations for making the earring are extensive, and include different ways to use the same technique on the necklace.

By dropping one bead off each row you will end up with a pyramid. Hang the fringe and add an ear wire, and you have created a uniquely different earring (see illustration).

For another different look, wrap the beaded square around a pencil and connect the two outside rows (shown), remove pencil, hang fringe, then string five beads and attach across the top for connecting the ear wire.

To change the appearance of the earring, simply change the color or cut of the beads. Try a color-lined crystal bead for a devastatingly elegant look, or use a teardrop crystal bead for the turn bead at the bottom of the fringe. I use a wide assortment of Austrian crystal beads to add highlights to many of the more expensive pieces of beadwork.

Working from the pyramid again, if you connect the two outside points, forming a circle, then to the remaining point, string a loop of five beads to which the ear wire is attached. From that same attachment point, hang one line of fringe down through the circle. Use a heavier bead for a turn bead at the bottom of the fringe to balance the earring. People will wonder how you created the effect it radiates, especially when done with a cut or crystal bead.

For a simple but elegant look, hang the beaded square from the top center row with the holes facing downward. Hang fringe from each bead row. You can string five beads into a loop at the top center for attaching the ear wire or attach the wire directly to the square if you prefer a shorter look.

Geometric designs, as well as floral and animal loomed patterns can be done with this weave. If it can be done on a loom, it can be done with this technique.

To make the loomed necklaces shown in the color pages, choose a loomed pattern for the center theme on the front piece. Follow the steps given for the earring square, except the piece will be larger.

Since you will be working up and down the pattern, bring the pattern across with each row. Begin on the left side of the pattern. Count the number of beads going down the first line, and string according to color the entire beginning row, as illustrated in step one.

The second row begins at the bottom and proceeds to the top. String the first two beads of the second row, and connect to the first row by passing the needle down through the second bead from the bottom of the first row (illustrated as step two). Continue connecting one bead at a time until the row is completed (as shown).

Bead row three exactly as row two, except from top to bottom.

With the completion of each row you will see the pattern begin to materialize. After completing the center piece, you will be ready to make the neckline pieces. For these smaller pieces use exactly one half of the pattern used for your center front piece, and make one half pattern for each side of the neckline as illustrated. You can use as many half pieces as you want on each side of the neckline, depending on the desired length.

When you begin the half pattern, if you are using the diamond pattern, the illustration shows how to drop a bead from each row in order to end up with a half diamond pattern.

To connect the center front piece to the neckline pieces, I have illustrated how to string and connect the strung beads from the center piece to each side of the neckline pieces.

This sounds like a very complicated technique, but if you will look closely at the illustrations, you will understand the simplicity of it.

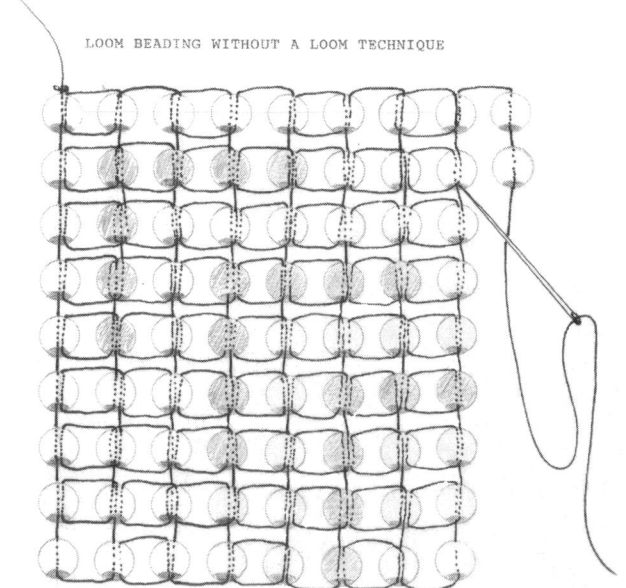

LOOM BEADING WITHOUT A LOOM TECHNIQUE

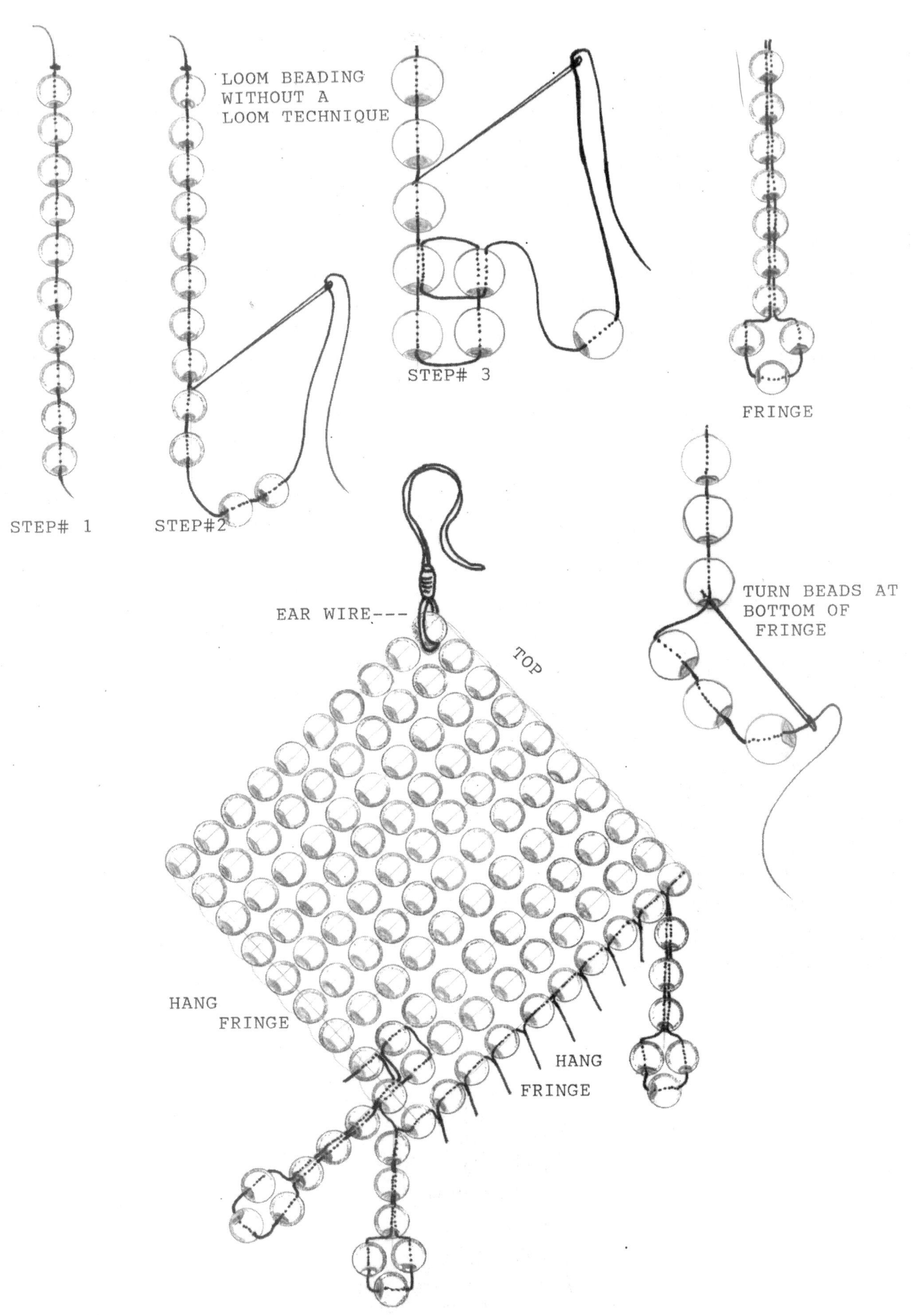

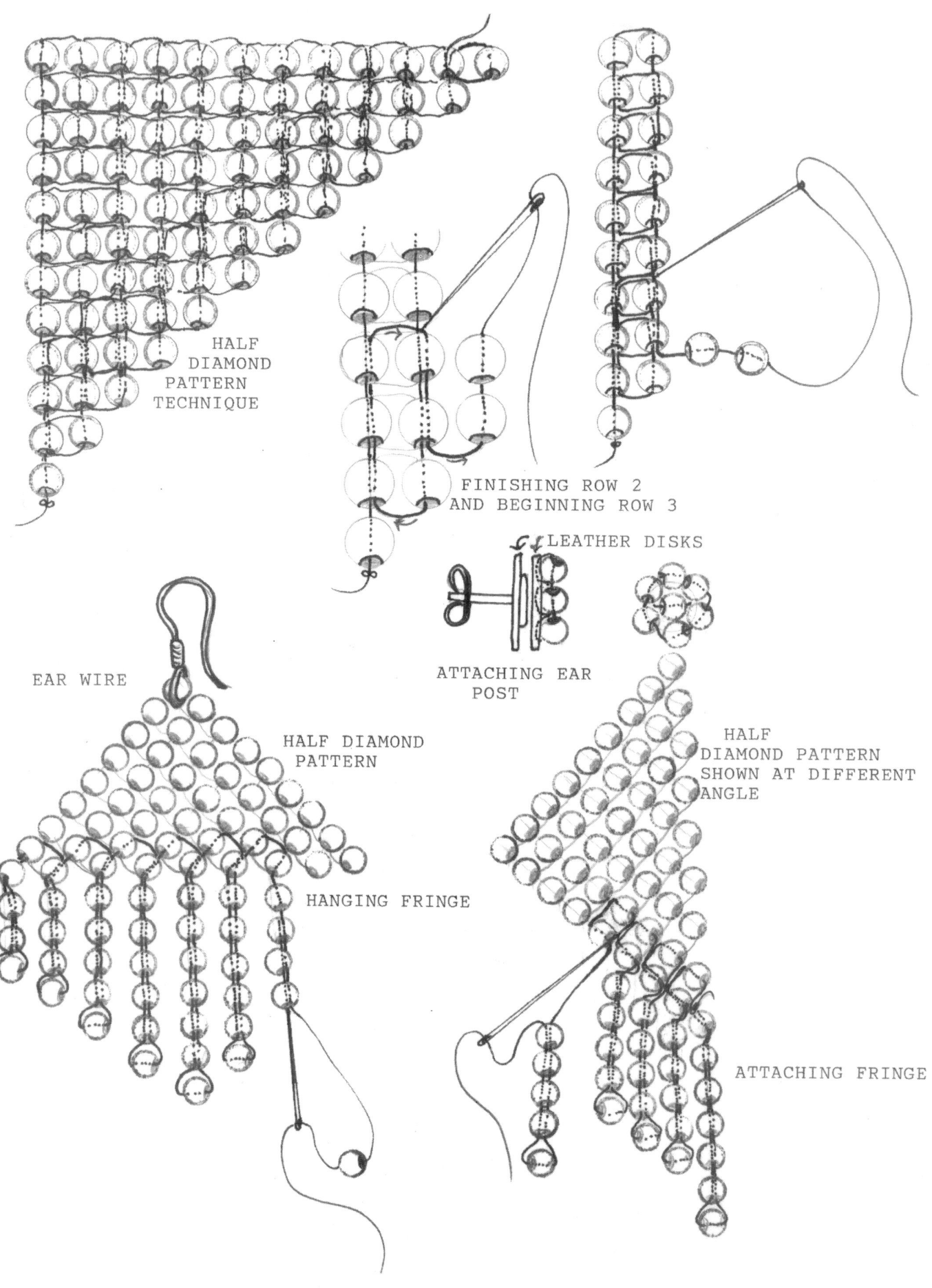

Connecting Front Center Theme to Neckline Piece

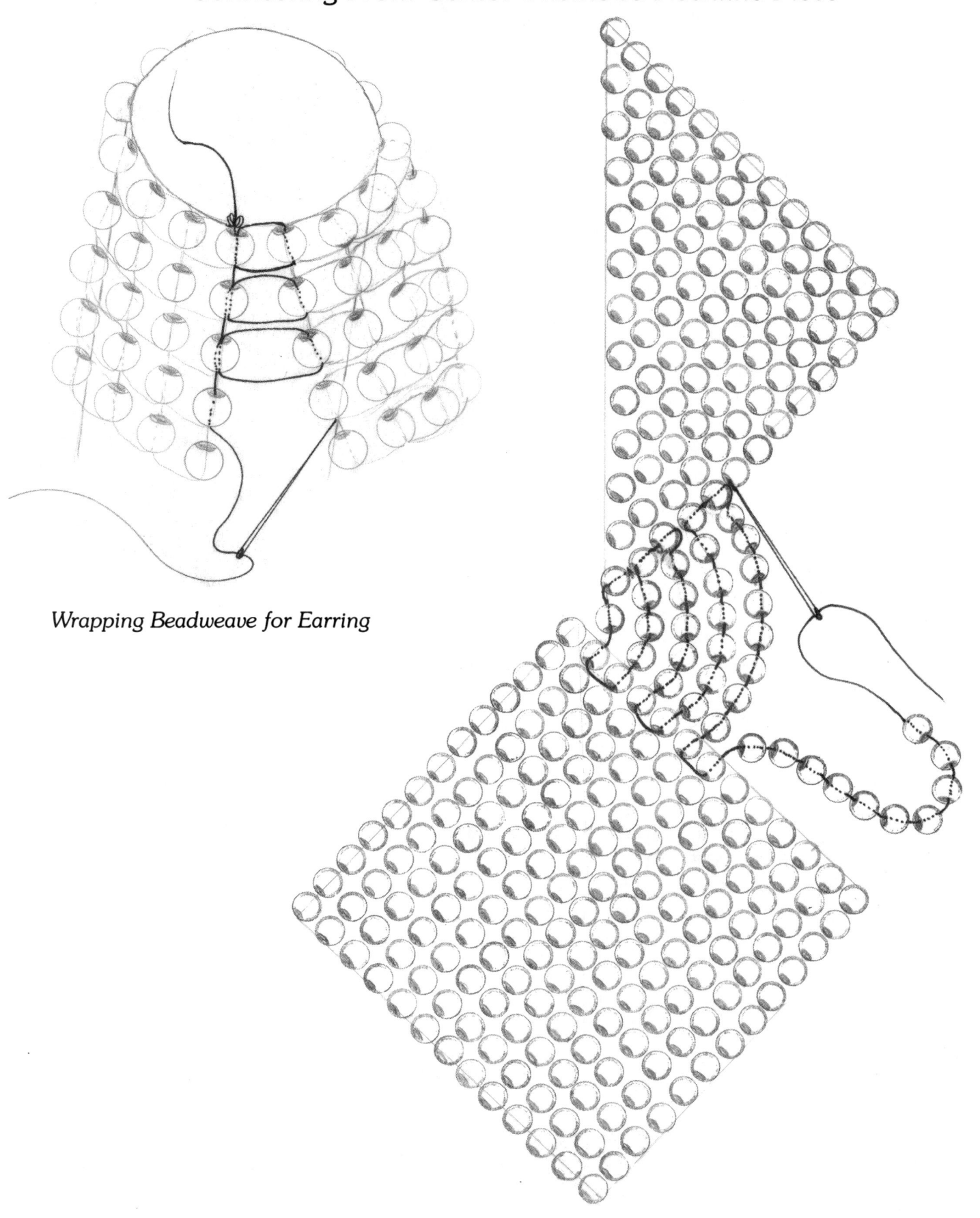

Wrapping Beadweave for Earring

Beaded Fringe

Beaded fringe makes a masterpiece of difference in the appearance of any ornament. It is a finishing touch that adds elegance or tradition, depending on the beaded pattern or the type of bead you use.

The elegant European costumes of the seventeenth and eighteenth centuries had lots of beaded fringe. The ladies' ball gowns shimmered because of the crystal seed bead fringe hanging all over them.

Every color, shape and size of glass seed bead was used for decorating the clothing of the very rich during those centuries. Elegance began and ended with the dainty little seed bead arranged in elaborate floral patterns.

More recently, in the early twentieth century, commonly referred to as the Roaring Twenties or flapper days, the seed bead business in the United States was again at its peak. Every woman who could sew on a button sewed seed beads on their garments. The beaded purse with long fringe was in demand and very stylish. Some of these purses are shown in the black and white photographs of this chapter. The ladies wore beaded head pieces, hair ornaments, dresses, shoes, coats or anything else that could be beaded. Lamp shades and curtains made of beads were the fashionable thing for the home decorator.

As you can see, the Native Americans were not the only people to be dazzled by the little seed bead. Beadwork and beaded fringe history belong to all generations, past and present, rich or poor. Every decade has its own fad involving beads, ranging from simple to extremely colorful to magnificently artful.

It is still a great year for bead designing.

Geometric necklace design, constructed using the switch back fringe technique, attached to a loomed strip for neckline. Author's.

Beaded fringe can be used to create the main body or theme of a pattern, as well as an added touch for trim. On the front cover of Volume One, I hung a deer's head in the fringe of the necklace. My sister-in-law, Doris Kennedy, has beaded the same necklace shown in the color pages of this volume. Any good beader should learn several fringing techniques and how to complement her beadwork and fringe with the right turn bead at the bottom of the fringe.

I have illustrated several types of fringes to stimulate your own imagination for color and uses. The geometric necklace shown in the black and white photo has been done with a switch back fringe attached to a loom beaded strip for the base. Don't forget, you don't need a loom to do these strips. Look at the loom beading without a loom technique.

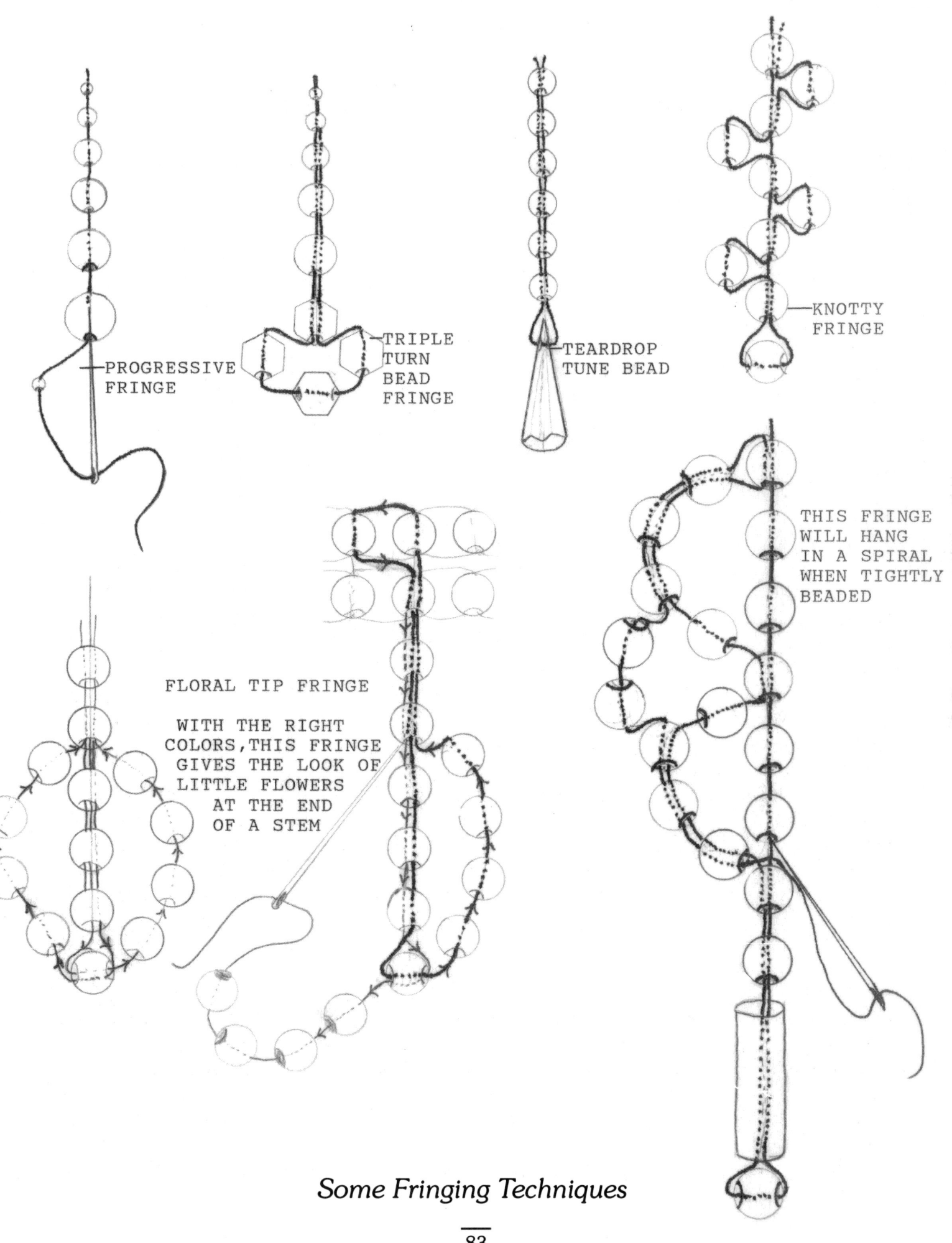

Some Fringing Techniques

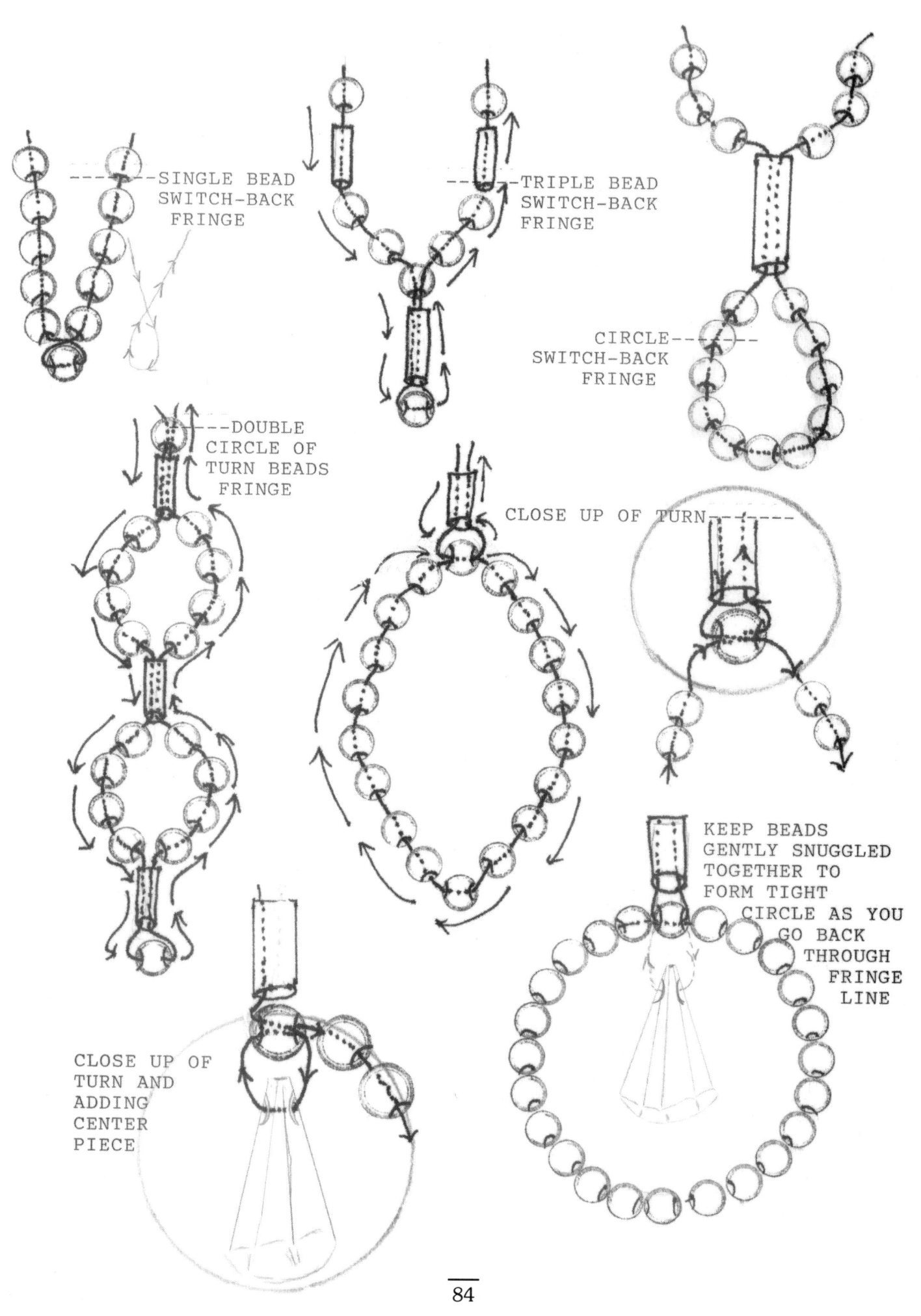

Beaded tomahawk, shown on hand-painted buffalo rug with a beaded medallion belt. Courtesy of Indian trading post, Mesa, Arizona.

Beaded knife scabbard, large nine-inch blade. Courtesy of Indian Trading Post, Mesa, Arizona.

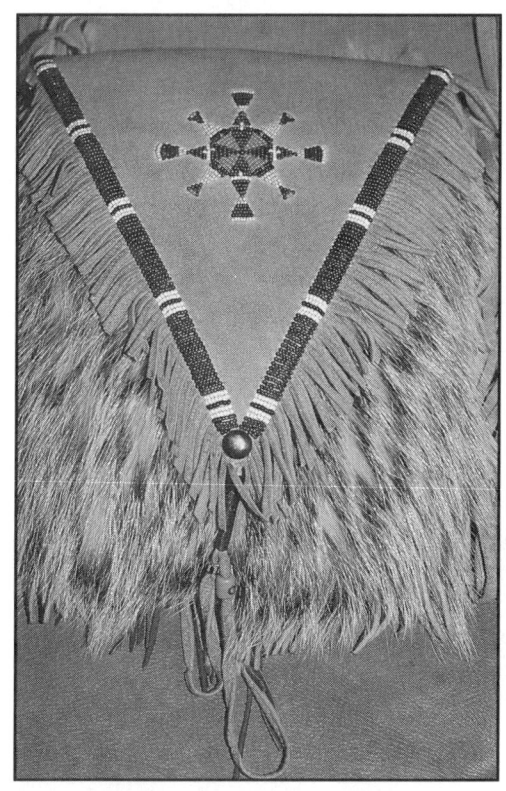

Beaded leather pouch with coyote trim. Courtesy of Greenriver Traders, Dubois, Wyoming.

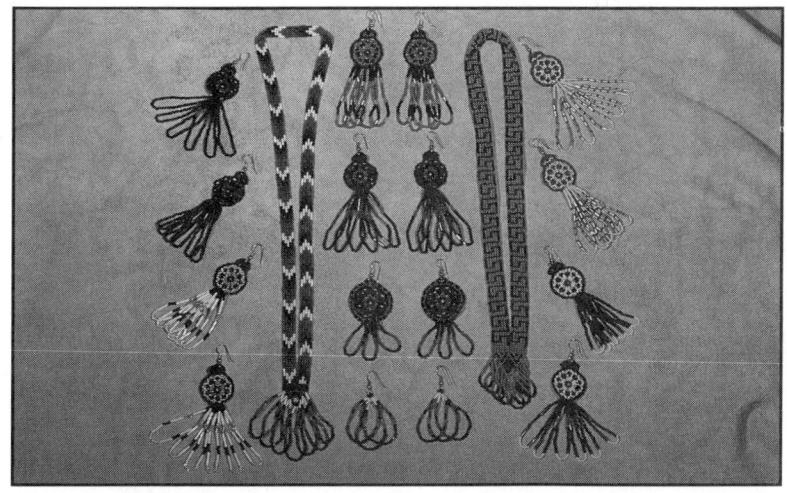

An assortment of Spanish lace earrings done by Sue St. Martin of Iron River, Wisc. Sue did the necklaces in this photo with the technique of "Loom Beading without a Loom."

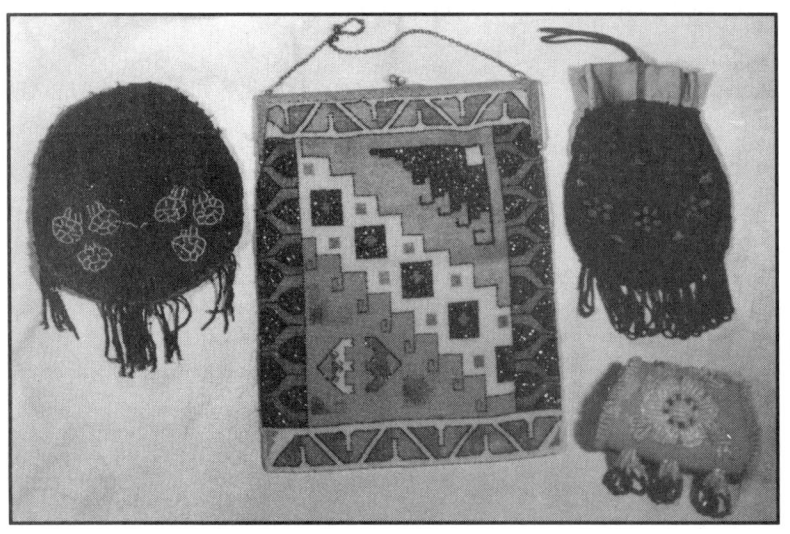

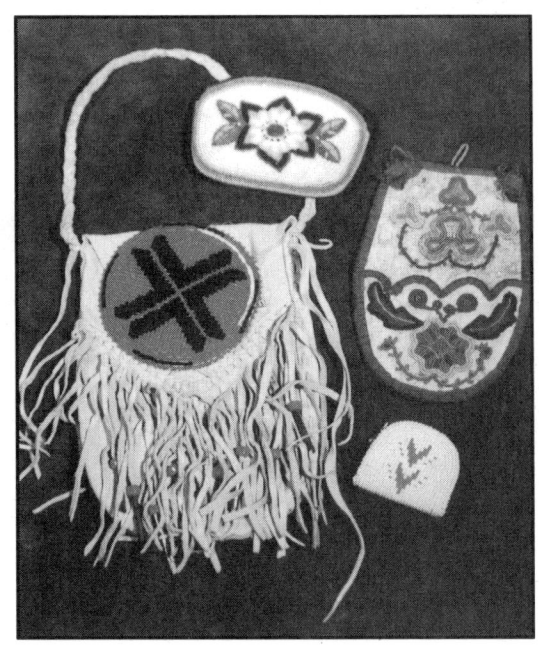

The purses shown on this page are considered antique. Most were made during the early Twentieth Century through the Roaring Twenties.

The white buckskin pouch is not antique. All of these items belong to the author.

The delicate patterns were done mainly in Europe, but sold in the U.S.A. Notice the large square purse done in Native American Indian design. The colors are brilliant blue, red, yellow and black with green border. This purse was made during the Eighteenth Century.

The geometric influence of the Indian design was received in the old world with great interest. Notice on the smaller white beaded purses the feathered circle, the geometric design and the war shield, with Shoshone flower.

The beaded jewelry on this page was designed by Jude Biegert, "The Bead Lady." Jude started to create grande garland necklaces in 1989. Each loomed necklace is backed with chamois and then attached to others by strung beads. The center front and back sections are fringed. She likes to work with nine-o, three-cuts and Swarovski crystal sun prisms.

Jude also designs embroidery lycra costumes for competitive skaters and dancers. She prefers to work with beads that play with light. I have shown another piece of Jude's work in the color section.

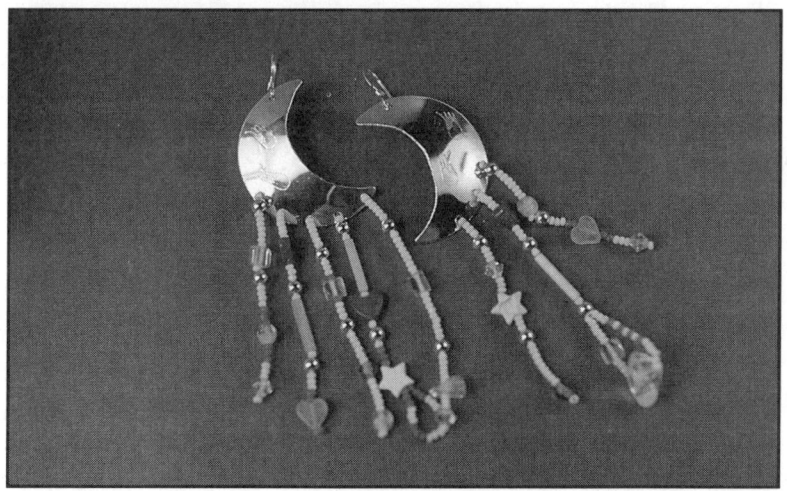

Instructions for the Beaded Belt Buckle

The beaded belt buckle has been a favorite with both men and women for years, especially those in the Western Dress Society. They are becoming more and more popular with the ladies now that the long beaded earrings are in fashion. She can have a belt buckle to match the earrings and moccasins to match the belt buckle.

In the color pages I have displayed some belt buckles done with animals that look like they have been painted rather than beaded. If you arrange your colors to reflect the natural colors of the animal or scenery and attach the beads in those sequences, the effect is quite painterly. A breathtaking array of jewelry can be done by "painting" with beads.

On the belt buckle illustration page I have given brief instructions on attaching the beaded front of the buckle to the metal buckle blank. In order to get a tight fit you must wet and stretch the leather before you sew the back of the buckle to the front. Sew the leather wet, and when finished, wet the back of the buckle again and spray with spray starch. Gently rub the spray starch into the leather and lay it in the sun to dry and shrink around the hook and metal belt loop.

Before you cut the slits for the metal loop and hook, lay the buckle down on the leather and press hard enough to make an impression in the wet leather exactly where the hook and loop are to be cut. This will take all the guesswork out.

If you have done your beadwork on felt, before you attach it to the back you should strengthen it by backing it with a piece of leather covering the stitches. This piece of leather should also be wet while you are working with it. As it dries along the back it will shrink slightly and make a good, tight-fitting buckle.

After you have sewed the back and front together with the buckle blank sandwiched in the center, sew an edge stitch around the edge to cover up the stitches.

When the leather has dried completely, your buckle is ready to wear. To make your moccasins match the belt buckle, bead two more front buckle pieces backed with leather and attach to the toe or side of your boot.

The Brick or Cheyenne Stitch

In the first two volumes of this series, I illustrated the brick stitch used in many different earring designs. There are no limits to the use of this weave. By extending the original pyramid, you can make belts or neckline pieces for any of the necklaces shown in the color pages that call for loomed strips. It is another weave that replaces the loom. Once you get the technique mastered, it can be done at a fast pace.

Another excellent use of this technique is shown in Shalimar Tracey's prize-winning necklaces shown in the color section of this volume. Shalimar has used a large pyramid and patterned small pyramids in the center of some necklaces. In others she connected pyramids, leaving an opening in the center shaped like a pyramid.

The method she used provides a beautifully planned effect. It differs, however, from the illustrated technique for extending pyramids. I cannot recall ever seeing the illustrated technique use by anyone but my mother and myself.

I have illustrated a simple stick-figure Indian village scene on the brick-stitch graph paper. Notice how it overlaps from one pyramid to another. You can continue to weave these pyramids together, following these steps for as long as you want with the pyramid size of your choice.

The brick-stitch graph paper illustrated here is available by writing to the publisher's address (send a self-addressed stamped envelope for information about the graph paper as well as a free list of stores that carry beading supplies) or by request from your local bead-carrying craft store. This graph paper can be used for the brick stitch when used sideways, and for the peyote stitch when used lengthwise.

Step-by-step illustrations of the brick-stitch will lead you from the beginning through the extending of the pyramids and show you how to drop a bead off to finish the piece.

For a variety of brick-stitch earring patterns, you will want to refer to volume two of Beads to Buckskins. If you have Peyote stitch earring patterns, they can easily be transposed to the brick-stitch.

SAMPLE PATTERN FOR EXTENDING THE BRICK STITCH PYRAMID

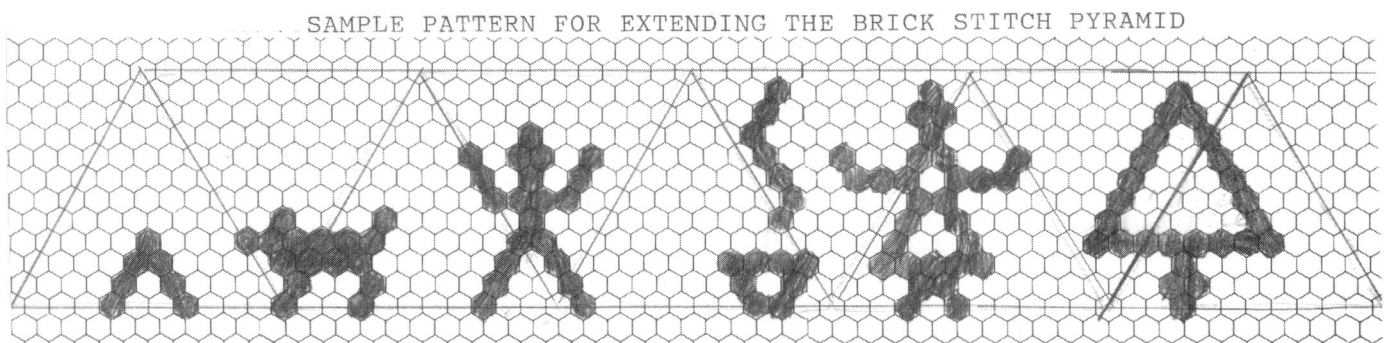

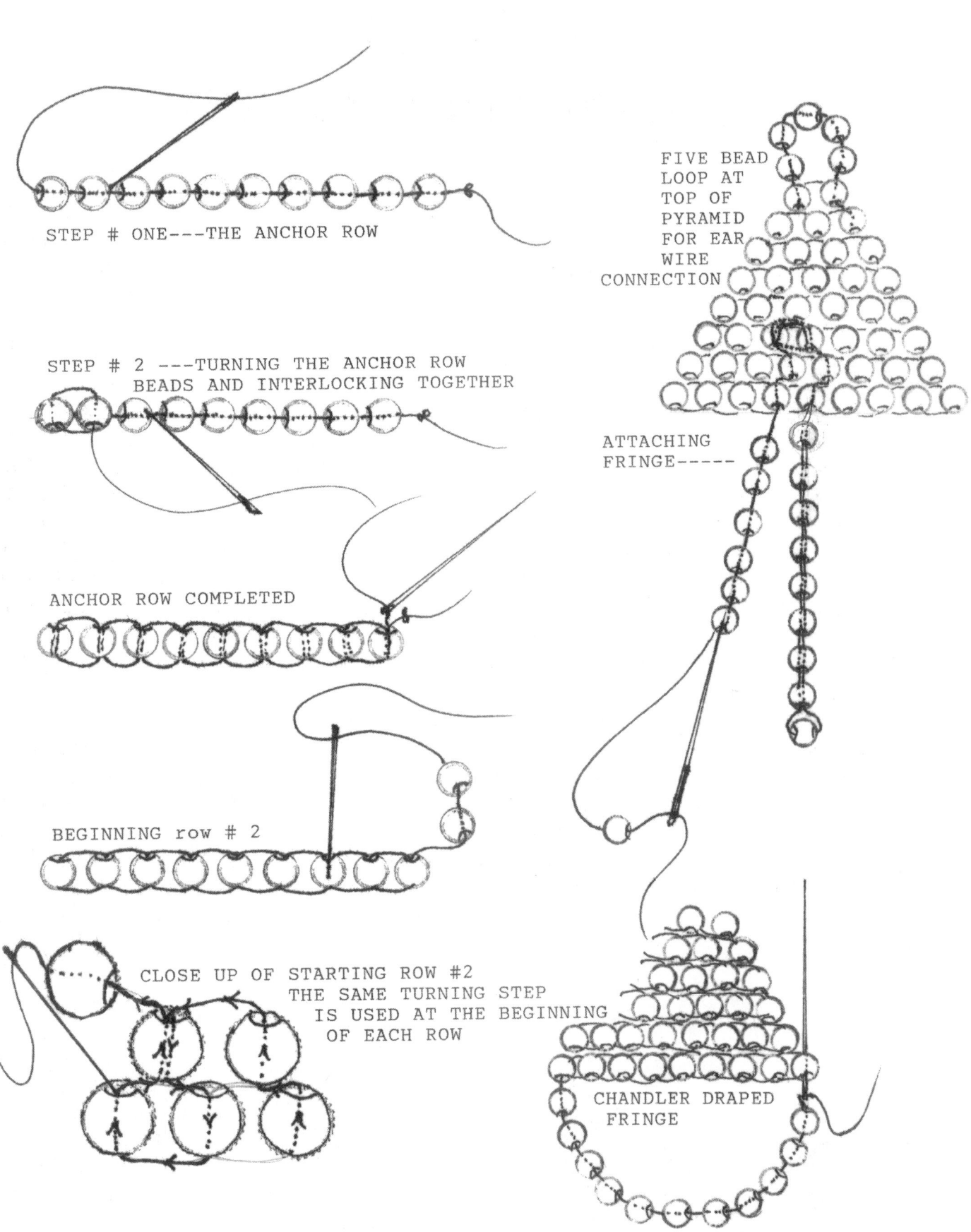

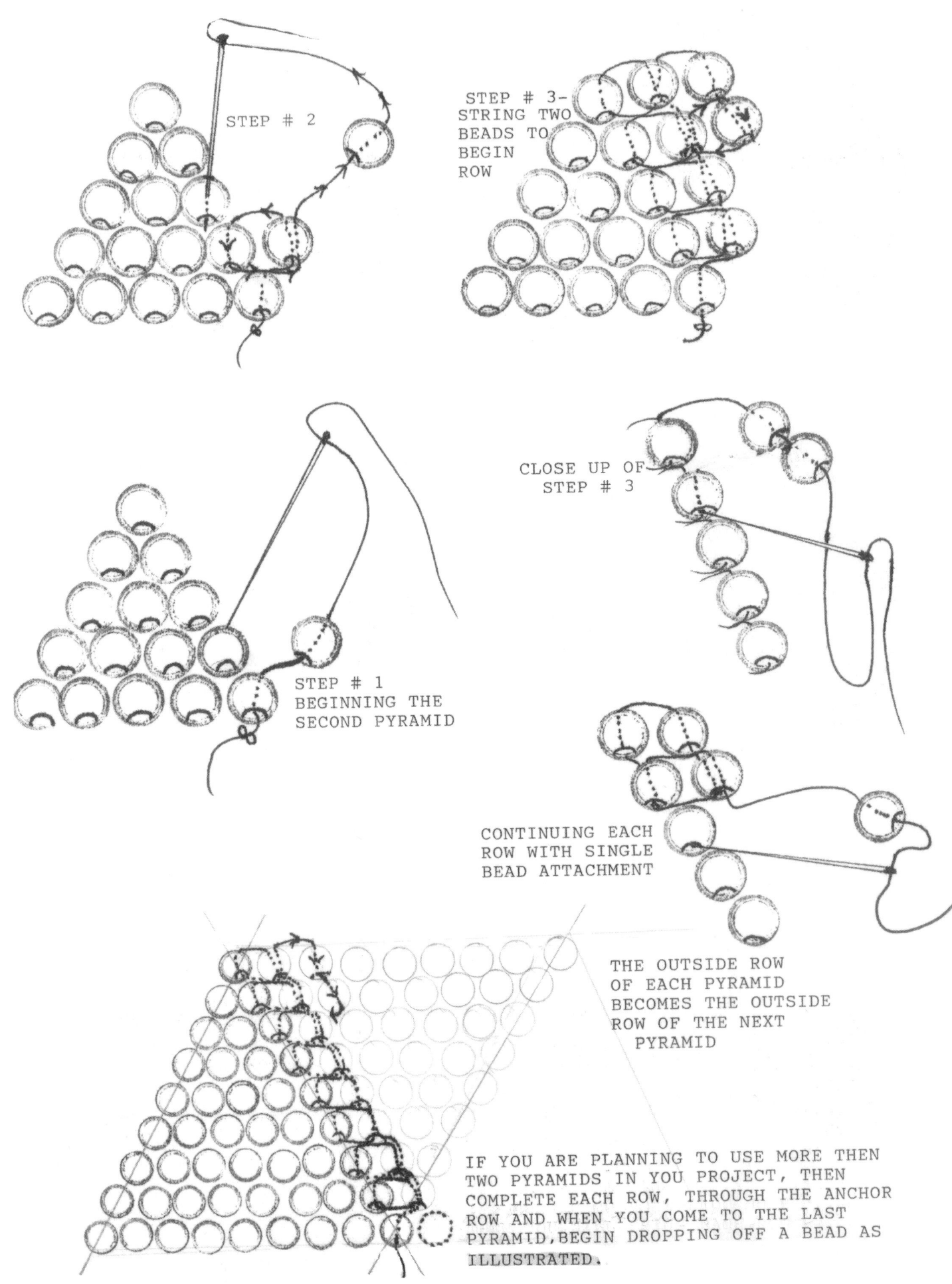

The Edge Stitch or Fretting

This important little technique doesn't receive much attention, but it has a certain place in almost every beading technique. Without a method to cover up the rough areas, our beadwork would look very amateur.

Edging, like any other needlework, is a matter of practice. That is why I repeat myself several times, stressing that the beginner start with a smaller project before attempting the intricate patterns displayed.

The edge stitch must harmonize in size and color coordination with the central theme of the piece. Many of the patterns shown in this volume call for an edge stitch or fret of some kind. An edge stitch that is too large overpowers the the object as a whole and dwarfs the basic theme. Try to keep the edge stitch as quietly subtle as possible. If you are covering a rough edge of leather hidden in the center of a piece of beadwork, you don't want to draw attention to it. On the other hand, if you are not hiding anything, then do something flowery and dainty that will focus attention on the center theme.

I like to use the edge stitch along each side of a loomed strip made for a lady's hat band. It provides a definite dainty look and separates the boys from the girls. The same can be done with purse straps, headbands, bracelets, barrettes and necklaces.

If you are a little artistic and can sketch or paint an animal or flower in a small buckskin circle, then do one of the edge stitches around it and hang an ear wire for an earring or make a necklace by arranging some neckline beads. Any number of things can be done with this technique.

The Native American Indians frequently edged their moccasins, pouches and garment seams with seed beads and porcupine quills.

The style for modern men of today is a ball cap beaded and edged around the front bill. For the ladies, edging an old felt western hat around the brim provides a fashionable look.

These are only a few suggestions for the use of this technique. For a completely different outlook about fretting, you will want to invest in volume four of Beads to Buckskins.

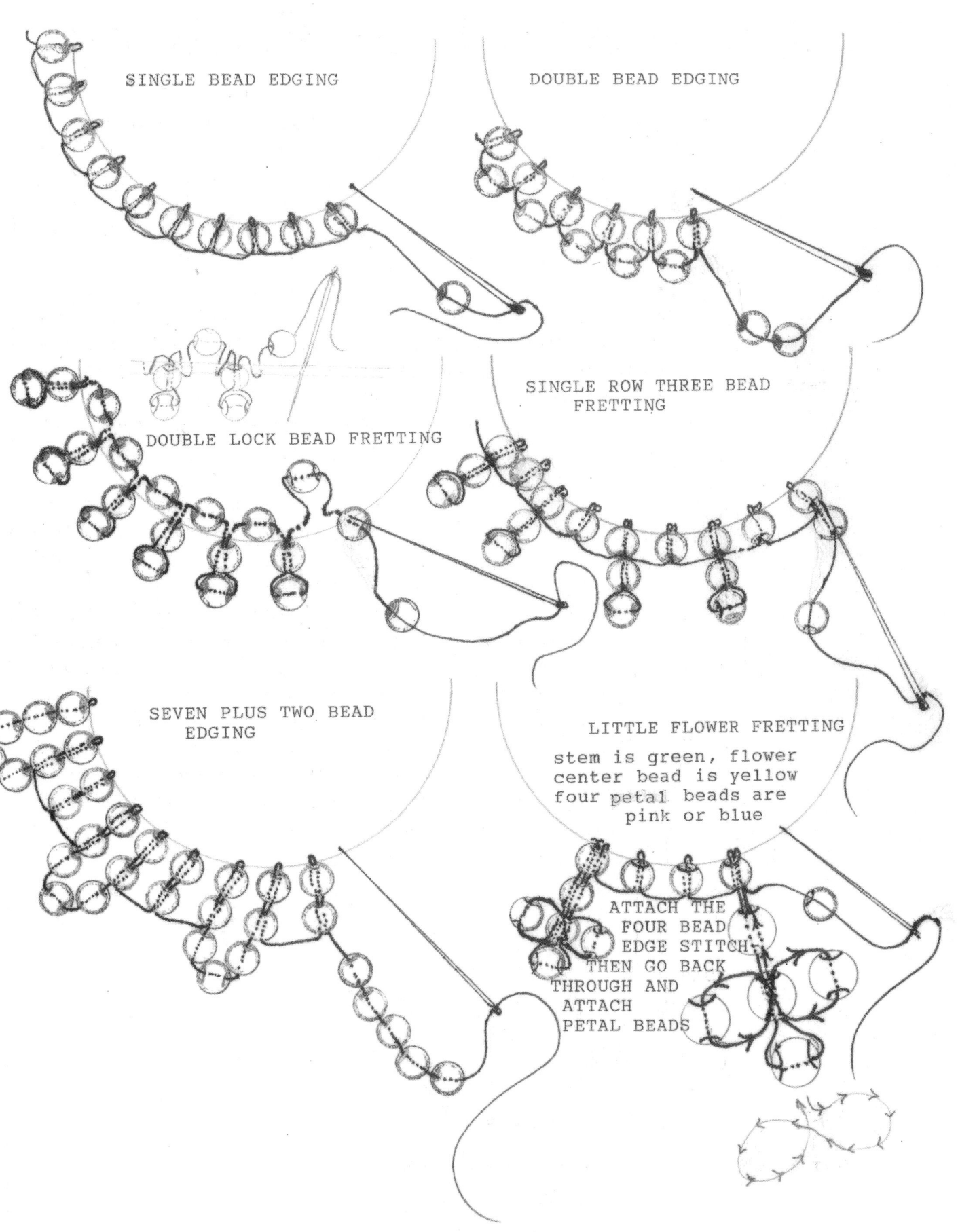